Traditions

Creating Memories to Draw Your Family Close

Kimberly L. Bytheway
Diane H. Loveridge

DESERET
BOOK

SALT LAKE CITY, UTAH

To all the rest of the "Loveridge Clan,"
who are each, individually, our best friends
and will be forever!

© 2003 Kimberly L. Bytheway and Diane H. Loveridge

Library of Congress Cataloging-in-Publication Data

Bytheway, Kimberly, 1975–
     Traditions : creating memories to draw your family close / Kimberly Loveridge Bytheway, Diane H. Loveridge.
          p.   cm.
     ISBN 1-59038-180-7 (Hardbound : alk. paper)
     1. Holidays.   2. Family.   I. Loveridge, Diane H.   II. Title.

GT3930.B98 2003
394.26—dc21   2003013420

Printed in the United States of America   72076
Publishers Printing
Salt Lake City, Utah

10   9   8   7   6   5   4   3

Contents

Creating a Happy Family 1

New Year's 3

Valentine's Day 12

Presidents' Day 19

St. Patrick's Day 21

First Day of Spring 25

April Fool's Day 28

Easter 32

Mother's Day 38

Memorial Day 42

Fourth of July 45

Pioneer Day 50

Back to School 54

Labor Day 59

Halloween 62

Veterans Day 68

Thanksgiving 72

Christmas Season 81

Christmas Eve 93

Fun with Santa Claus 99

Christmas Day 102

Scripture Study 108

Mealtime 114

Baptism 118

Twelfth Birthday 122

Mission and Temple Endowment 125

Sunday Activities 129

At Work in the Home 134

Vacations 141

Birthdays 153

General Family Fun 163

Family Harmony and Getting Along 176

Television and Computer 180

Bedtime 183

A Nontraditional Afterthought 187

Creating a Happy Family

We feel that happy families don't just happen by accident or luck—they are created. Bonds can exist between family members that will be a joy and a strong support in good times and bad. But just because people are related to each other doesn't mean that they have good relationships. Those bonds have to be forged through hours spent together in meaningful activities and traditions. How will a family draw closer if they have not spent time together creating memories and sharing good moments with one another?

President Gordon B. Hinckley has said, "I believe our problems, almost every one, arise out of the homes of the people. If there is to be a reformation, if there is to be a change, if there is to be a return to old and sacred values, it must begin in the home. It is here that truth is learned, that integrity is cultivated, that self-discipline is instilled, and that love is nurtured" (*Ensign,* November 1998, 97).

As parents, we want to pass our values and priorities on to our children. We want them to cherish the same goodness that we treasure. We want our children to turn to the family during troubled times, and not to other outside sources. This is the meaning of parenthood: to teach our children to love one another and to live the gospel. They will not learn this by accident, but in the quiet, planned moments, purposefully taught.

This is where meaningful family traditions come in. When we spend time together as a family, month after month, season after season, and year after year, we strengthen the central unit of the gospel: the family. In a day when the family is under attack from the most sophisticated sources ever devised, this responsibility becomes paramount.

Family traditions are for everyone. They don't have to be elaborate or expensive. They don't have to involve huge groups. Even simple activities can bring the family together to create memories and promote feelings of love.

We realize that every family is different, and our goal is simply to give you a whole variety of ideas in the hopes that there will be a few that you can use, or that will help to spark your own creativity, to bring your family closer and to make your relationships stronger. That is what traditions are all about. It isn't necessarily *what* you do, but simply that you do something.

New Year's

When New Year's is mentioned in our family, there is an immediate excitement in the air because we have always tried to make a big deal of this holiday. It just seems to start the year out right when we share this time as a family. We go the extra mile in the planning to make it an especially successful and fun event, and consequently, everyone plans on attending and looks forward to that time together.

PROGRESSIVE DINNER

If you have extended family nearby, have a progressive dinner. Begin with hors d'oeuvres at one home, then move on to the next home for appetizers. Travel from one home to another until all the courses of dinner are completed. If you have only a few places to visit, combine courses. You can make this as casual or as fancy as you want. Dress in sequins, or come in jeans. Serve on china, or use your plastic silverware. Serve shrimp or burgers. Adapt to your family's own sense of style.

YEAR-END FAMILY QUIZ

Keep a notebook in a handy spot in your house, and throughout the year write down special events and moments that family members have. On New Year's, have a quiz about the events of the past year and give prizes to the family members who can answer the most questions correctly.

FIREWORKS SHOW

Purchase fireworks to be lit off expressly at midnight on New Year's Eve. Use sparklers if you want to be quiet, or fountains for a more spirited event. Invite extended family to participate. It adds an extra bit of excitement for the children to look forward to if they can stay awake until the stroke of twelve, and the neighbors always seem to join in the fun!

New Year's Toast

Add a special touch to your midnight celebration with some sparkling apple juice in fancy goblets. Toast the new year and drink together as the clock chimes it in. Then take turns toasting special events of the past year and hopes for the year to come.

Make Resolutions!

At midnight, have a pencil and paper ready to write down your New Year's resolutions. Make them simple enough that you will truly keep them. Then, share with those around you what you have written. When all in the family know your goals, you can call upon them for added support when you feel tempted to let your resolutions lapse!

Personality Portrait

Have your family portrait taken, including extended family if possible. Family members could each dress in a way that reflects something special to them about the past year—maybe a costume from a play they participated in, a uniform from a sport they played, a graduation cap and gown—or they could carry a musical instrument they worked on during the year. Each year, try to find something different to highlight, and as you look through the pictures in the future you will look back on many different years of accomplishments.

We Wish You a Merry New Year

To minimize some of the time constraints of Christmas, send a New Year's letter to friends and family rather than a Christmas card to highlight your past year of events. Include a family portrait to show how your family has grown. When sent after the Christmas rush, it is sure to be a nice surprise for friends and family who weren't expecting it.

Family Game Day

Get together for a full day of games and food. Start as early as you want, and play late into the night or even into the wee hours of the morning. Have each family member choose a game and make sure that all games are played. Have lots of snacks and treats to last as long as you do!

Shop 'Til You Drop

Instead of giving new clothes at Christmas, start the new year out with a clothing shopping spree together. Wait for the after-Christmas sales and then hit all of your favorite stores. Have a contest to see who can find the best bargains. Take a break for lunch together before heading out again. Later that evening, model your new fashions together at a family fashion show. Finish off with family foot rubs to ease tired feet after the event.

$\mathcal{L}$ET ME GUESS

Sit down together as a family and have each member write down one thing that they would like to improve or work on during the following year. This should be a character trait or habit that is apparent to others. Seal them in envelopes and tuck them safely away in a common place, to be opened the following year. Before each person opens his or her envelope on the following New Year's Eve, have the other family members try to guess what that improvement has been. It will be fun to see what improvements others have noticed, as perhaps you have grown in more areas than just one. This will be a very positive experience, and might help the longevity of New Year's resolutions.

$\mathcal{N}$EW YEAR ANGEL

"In an effort to help our children keep the excitement and happiness of the holidays, and also to encourage them to behave, we created the 'New Year Angel.' We hold back a gift from the Christmas gifts and save it to be given on New Year's Eve. The gift is left at the foot of their bed or by their door before they wake in the morning. It creates a delightful excitement, plus it helps us get along during the time we spend together during the already stressful season."

—CheRee Tanner

Family Slide Show

Each New Year's, have family members choose a few of their favorite pictures from the past year and highlight them in an annual family slide show. Invite as many extended family members as possible, and gather together for a night of popcorn eating, laughing, and reminiscing. Use background music to enhance the "show" that each person chooses for his or her segment of the program.

Midnight Phone Call

"Every year at midnight, we expect a phone call from Mom, the first to wish us a 'Happy New Year.'"

—Diane Bytheway

Ladies' Day Out

If the men in your family enjoy watching football games on New Year's Day, the women might like to plan activities of their own such as bowling, ice-skating, or going to a movie.

Dear Me

Every year, write a letter to yourself about the things you would like to accomplish during the following year. Seal the envelope and put it in a safe place. Open it next year on New Year's and see how you did before writing yourself another letter.

New Year's "Nerdie"

"Every New Year's Eve we have had our children place one shoe by the fireplace. They were told at Christmastime that if they had taken good care of their toys and been good children, Mrs. Santa Claus, alias 'Nerdie,' would put a treat in their shoe that night. On New Year's Day, when they awakened, they would find something in their shoe. Now our children are doing it with their children. For as long as we can remember, all the Bowen children have put out their shoes before going to bed on New Year's Eve and hoped Nerdie would fill them before morning. Each generation has wondered why we were lucky enough to have Little Nerdie when so many of their friends had never even heard of her!"

—Bruce and René Bowen

Time Capsule

"In our family, we really look forward to the 'time capsule.' It is buried out in Grandpa's backyard. Every seven years, we dig it up and read predictions and goals, look at pictures and drawings, and listen to audiotapes we made seven years earlier. We then sit down and add to the capsule our new pictures and drawings and recordings. Then we bury it again and wait seven years until we can dig it up and see how we have all grown."

—Jann Cahoon

FAMILY HOME NEW YEAR'S EVENING

"For New Year's Eve we enjoy staying at home with our children. We always fix a delicious meal and then spend the rest of the evening playing all kinds of games."

—Merete Sorensen, Sandra Cannon

BANGING IN THE NEW YEAR

"As a family, we always bring in the new year by banging on pots and pans and running through the streets of the neighborhood making as much noise as possible!"

—Julie Knapp Meyer

NEW FACES FOR THE NEW YEAR

On New Year's Day, have a family makeover. You can go to a professional salon or simply stay at home and use your own skills to give each other a new look to celebrate a new year. Start with facials and manicures. Then try a new hairdo, experiment with a different hair color, or just see the changes makeup can make. Be sure to take "before and after" photos to capture the dramatic differences.

FOR THE SPORTS FAN

"At our house we all enjoy sports, especially football on New Year's Day. We watch all of the games and fix an easy but delicious dinner of steak, roast, or baked chicken."

—Judy Baadsgaard

New Year's Mug

"A tradition in our family has been to set out a mug on the fireplace hearth every New Year's Eve for each child in the family. Then on New Year's morning, the mug has been filled with candy and a small gift left by 'Tippy Toes' or 'The Little New Year.'"

—Konnie Peterson

Mother Goose Day

"After Christmas we look forward to New Year's Eve. Before we go to bed, we all put out our hats so that Mother Goose can drop us a present. On the morning of Mother Goose Day (New Year's Day) all of us check our hats for a little surprise."

—Randi Nuila

Valentine's Day

From the youngest to the oldest in our family, we love this romantic, happy holiday when we can express love and appreciation to those close to us. We try to focus our attention on others, doing service and sharing joy, and we always receive great joy in return.

Heart-Shaped Cookie Bake

Each Valentine's Day, gather your family for a cookie bake. Make a huge batch of cookie dough and shape it into large cookies, the size of dinner plates. As each cookie comes out of the oven, have a child decorate it however he or she chooses and then put a friend's name in the center of the cookie. It will be fun for the children to use their own creativity for their friends and to see what the others are creating. When the cookies are ready, drive around together to deliver them to the friends. Back at home, shape the rest of the dough for the children to make cookies for themselves.

Love from Mom and Dad

On Valentine's Day, make sure that everyone in the family wakes up to a special valentine from Mom and Dad. This is especially fun if Dad can give a gift to his daughters, and Mom to her sons. For example, each daughter might wake up to a single rose in her bedroom along with a love note from Dad, and the sons awaken to a small box of chocolates with a love note from Mom.

Hidden Valentines

Hide valentines throughout your home in strategic places where they will be found at different times by your family members throughout the day. Put some in the bathroom, in the refrigerator, in the cars, and even in the beds for a good-night wish.

Valentine Breakfast

Make Valentine's Day special for your family by making a valentine breakfast. Color pancake batter red and cook it into heart shapes. Cut the butter into heart shapes, and make the milk pink. Use a heart-shaped cookie cutter to make valentine toast. Serve the breakfast with strawberries. (Their shape looks much like a heart.) Use special napkins with hearts on them. Your family will appreciate this loving touch to the morning.

Love Container

Buy a little heart-shaped container that can hold some type of candy or note. At the beginning of the month, show the heart to the family. Fill it and give it to someone else in the family when no one is watching. It is then that person's turn to fill the container and secretly pass it along to someone else. Enjoy the month of February watching the "love container" pass throughout the whole family again and again.

School Surprise

Because children get so excited about delivering their valentines to their friends, surprise them by having a valentine given to them at school—special delivery. Include balloons if you wish, or just send a favorite little treat. They are sure to enjoy the surprise and the message of love.

VALENTINE PICNIC

"One Valentine's Day, I put off making dinner reservations until I couldn't find a restaurant anywhere with any availability. So, when the time came to go out, I told my wife to go upstairs and get ready for the evening. When she came downstairs, I had decorated the living room with some of our houseplants and a checkered picnic blanket on the floor. I filled a picnic basket and put on a CD of outdoor sounds. We had a memorable picnic dinner right there on the floor, and it has become a favorite tradition. When the children came along, we included them, so now we all look forward to our 'Valentine Picnic.'"

—John Bytheway

VALENTINE FAMILY HOME EVENING

"On the Sunday or Monday before Valentine's Day, we have a special family home evening lesson on the subject of love. We go around the circle and give reasons why we love each member of the family."

—Marion Clark

HOME DECORATING

Decorate your home for Valentine's Day. Buy some red lightbulbs to replace the white ones in your lamps, or wrap red cellophane around the light fixtures to create a "red room." Use crepe paper and balloons to add to the effect. Set aside a time when the children can help create this valentine atmosphere.

A Valentine to Snack By

Surprise your family by sending valentine cards to them in their lunches. Use colored construction paper and include some little valentine treats for them to eat. Write love messages to let them know that you are thinking of them.

Remember the Widows

Sit together at the table and make special valentines for the widows in your neighborhood. Talk about the specific people and try to decorate the valentines according to what you think they like. Draw pictures of special talents they have, and write a note inside wishing them a happy Valentine's Day.

Dinner Plate Valentine

When setting the dinner table on Valentine's Day, turn the dinner plates upside down. Hide little treasures under the overturned plates, such as jewelry, candy, or notes. This will be an exciting way for your family members to get a valentine from you.

My Sleepy Little Valentine

Many stores sell pajamas decorated with hearts and other valentine symbols. For Valentine's Day, get some new sleepwear and set it out on the family's beds. When it is time to retire for the night, each one will be surprised at the final valentine of the day awaiting them.

*L*OVE IN ANY LANGUAGE

In the weeks before Valentine's Day, have each family member pick a foreign language and practice a few phrases that might come in handy for Valentine's Day. For family home evening one night you could take turns teaching one another how to say "I love you," "You're the best," and "Thank you" in these different languages. On Valentine's Day, practice your "phrases of love" with one another in any foreign language that comes to mind.

*C*ANDLELIGHT DINNER FOR ALL

Make the traditional romantic candlelight dinner a family event. Have everyone dress up in their finest clothes and sit down at an elegant table, complete with place cards, cloth napkins, goblets, and silver. Serve the dinner "restaurant style" with nicely arranged plates complete with parsley. Try to have everyone use proper manners, as if they were at a fancy restaurant.

*T*HE "LOVE WALL"

Cut out a bunch of red paper hearts and place them in a basket by the door. Every time a person does a kind deed for someone else, have the person write it down on a heart and tape it onto the wall. It will amaze you how quickly the wall will fill with "love," and how excited family members will become as they anticipate their next service to contribute to the wall.

HEART ATTACK

Give your family members a "heart attack." In other words, "attack" their bedroom, car, desk, locker, or office with hearts. Cut out dozens of hearts and sneak to cover your chosen spot with them. You can add a bag of candy sprinkled on the floor for a little extra fun. Write a note telling them that they have just had a "heart attack."

Presidents' Day

This often-overlooked holiday has become an important part of our family's traditions as we have learned more about the great men who have served and led our country to become the force for good that it is today. We have gained a deep and abiding respect for these leaders and look forward to honoring them on their holiday.

Birthday Party

Celebrate Presidents' Day with a typical birthday party for George Washington and Abraham Lincoln. Have birthday cake and ice cream, and sing songs about the presidents, as well as "Happy Birthday."

Presidential Reports

Learn about why we celebrate Presidents' Day, and about the specific contributions Abraham Lincoln and George Washington made to the development of our country. Have the children study and then give reports on these great men. Try acting out some of their character traits in skits performed for extended family members.

Letters to the President

Take time to learn more about the current president of our country. Read newspaper articles to gather information about his life, family, and beliefs. Write letters to him and express gratitude for some of the things you appreciate about his leadership.

Cherry Pie Delivery

"We dressed up our children in colonial costumes on Presidents' Day and delivered cherry pies to welcome in some new neighbors. We had no idea what impact the experience would have on our otherwise reserved and typically private neighbors. They started talking to each other, having parties, and enjoying each other's company."

—Cynthia Dayton

St. Patrick's Day

Having some Irish blood has certainly influenced the way we celebrate this holiday, but you don't need to be Irish to jump in and fully enjoy the great traditions of Ireland. Everyone in your family can look forward to this "green-letter" day as they anticipate the annual traditions.

ℒᴜᴄᴋʏ Bʀᴇᴀᴋꜰᴀsᴛ

For breakfast, make "green shamrock" pancakes. Cut out enough paper shamrocks for each family member, making just one with four leaves instead of three. Place the shamrocks under the breakfast plates. Just before eating, have your family look under their plates. The "lucky" one with the four-leaf clover gets to say the prayer on the food or receives some other type of reward. Then go around the table and have each person tell some way that they feel they are "lucky," or, as we prefer to say it, blessed.

𝒜 Lɪᴛᴛʟᴇ Gʀᴇᴇɴ ꜰᴏʀ Dɪɴɴᴇʀ

Serve an entirely green dinner. Rice can be turned a particularly bright shade of green! Eat salad, green gelatin, and kiwi fruit. (Truly, anything can be made green if you use enough food coloring.) Put one little drop of green food coloring in the bottom of each person's glass, and watch the surprise as the beverage being poured suddenly turns green!

ℰɢɢ Dᴇᴄᴏʀᴀᴛɪɴɢ

You can decorate eggs for any holiday! For St. Patrick's Day, spend time as a family dipping and decorating eggs in different shades of green. Get creative with beads and feathers, and have a contest to see who can come up with the most unusual egg.

Home Decorations

Decorate your home with as much green as you can. You can buy green lightbulbs or use green cellophane to get the desired effect. Have the whole family dress in as much green as possible, and reward the person who comes up with the most green. (Some may even get creative enough to color tongues and nails green!)

Irish Video

Check out a video from your local library about Ireland, or a movie set in Ireland. Watch as a family, and learn more about the culture and landscape of the beautiful countryside. Snack on green food.

School at the End of the Rainbow

"I liked to deliver secretly a pot of gold (a black, plastic witch's cauldron filled with gold-wrapped chocolate coins) to my child's classroom on St. Patrick's Day."

—Lynnell King

Leprechaun Chores

Send your children on a treasure hunt to find the pot of gold left behind by a leprechaun. In each room, have your children complete a chore that the "naughty leprechaun" has left undone. When the task is complete, give them the next clue to lead them to the next chore. At the end of the adventure, reward them with chocolate gold coins, sucker rings, and candy necklaces.

THE DINING IRISH

Cook a traditional Irish dinner for your family. Look in recipe books to create original dishes from Ireland. Teach your family about some of the traditions observed in Ireland, and show them the typical ancient dress of the country. During dinner, speak in Irish accents for fun, or begin every word with *o.* (For example: "O'Carrie o'is o'sleeping.")

First Day
of Spring

Spring is exciting and full of wonder as we anticipate the first crocuses and tulips pushing up
through the ground. We have loved sharing this
special event as a family, both old and young, as
we come together to appreciate the miracle of
growth and rebirth.

Plant a Garden

Take time to plant a garden. Explain to your family about the gifts Heavenly Father has given us in the beautiful growth all around us. Give each child a section of the garden to take care of all by himself or herself, and teach them the basics about water and sunlight. See their delight as they enjoy the fruits of their labors.

Spring De-Junking Day

Have a "spring cleaning" day. Let each member of the family gather a pile of items to give away to charity. Spend the entire day together cleaning the garage, de-junking bedrooms, or just deep-cleaning the kitchen and bathrooms. Prepare the ground for planting. After a hard day of work, enjoy a picnic or other rewarding activity together.

Snow Picnic

"Every spring before the snow has melted from the high mountains, our family takes a drive to have a snow picnic. We take large garbage bags and go snow body surfing. It is always so beautiful, and we always get sunburned. After playing in the snow, we eat our picnic lunch."

—Claudia Kimball Miles

Visit the Zoo

Spring is a wonderful time to celebrate new life. If you live near a zoo or aviary, call ahead and see if any of the animals have recently delivered babies. Take a trip to see the new creatures. As you're driving, discuss the miracle of new life and the blessing of birth for all of God's creations.

Plant a Tree

Whether your yard needs it or not, purchase a tree together and find an area of your neighborhood to beautify. It may be a park or a neighbor's home, and your family members will certainly enjoy knowing that they helped beautify the landscape with their own labors.

April Fool's Day

Our family loves April Fool's Day because we like pulling good-natured pranks and jokes. It's the one time of year we can get away with being just a little bit mischievous. We have grown closer together as we have learned to laugh at each other—and especially at ourselves, when some-one has successfully tricked us!

Meal Mix-Up

Try mixing up the meals of the day. Serve hamburgers at breakfast time and eggs and bacon for dinner. When the day starts with a wacky breakfast, the children are certain to catch on quickly to the holiday . . . in case they forgot!

Strange Sock Show

Have an annual "strange sock" day. Find a discount or dollar store and have each person buy a strange pair of socks. Model the purchases in a home fashion show and reward the person with the most "foolish" pair.

Best Bargain Presents

Draw names of family members before heading out to the store. Have each person spend a given amount on the person whose name he or she drew, finding the "best bargain" possible for the recipient. Go home and exchange gifts, deciding together who actually got the most for their dollar.

Unique Hat Contest

Spend some time together making strange hats. Use construction paper or old hats from the costume box. Accent with sequins, paper cups, feathers, and beads. After everyone has completed his or her "crowning glory," go out on the town and see what the public thinks. Watch others' strange reactions to your new accessories!

Unusual Dinner Party

Have a strange foods party. Eat things that you wouldn't normally eat, such as lemons, green olives, and sardines. Take instant pictures just as each person takes a bite of the unaccustomed food, and then laugh at the photographed reactions.

Chocolate-Dipped Everything

Dip many different foods in chocolate. Have each person bring a different food to the chocolate pot and dip it in secret. Then go around the table, have everyone try one of the selections, and see if you can guess (without looking) what you are eating.

Bizarre Fashion Show

Give everyone a price limit, and go to a nearby used clothing store. Spend time shopping together, picking out the most peculiar outfits you can find. Either go home with your new clothes to show off to one another, or head out together for dinner and a night on the town.

Crazy Colored Food

Go crazy with food coloring! Color your milk pink, or turn your cookies blue. Have each member of the family use a different color and see how many different colors you can include in your meals.

GAG-GIFT EXCHANGE

Have a silly gag-gift exchange. Each person brings a humorous gift, nicely wrapped. Draw numbers to see who gets to choose first from the pile of gifts. The first person chooses a gift but does not open it. Then the second person chooses, and so on, until every person has a gift. Open all the gifts at once and see what "treasures" each person has acquired.

Easter

Our family has come to appreciate the unique nature of this holiday, combining the reverence of the resurrection of the Savior with the fun and mystery of the Easter Bunny. We love planning activities that encompass both aspects of Easter, and have grown closer through the spiritual as well as the secular.

Easter Egg Hunt

Have a traditional Easter egg hunt. You can do this several different ways depending on the dynamics of your family. You might have the family gather all of the candy they've found into one large pile to be divided equally, or perhaps you might have each family member gather only one specific color of plastic egg, making sure that there are equal amounts of each color. Some families hide entire Easter baskets and have the family members search for their own. Any way you do it, the family is sure to have fun finding what the Easter Bunny has left behind.

Confetti Eggs

Poke small holes in both ends of raw eggs and blow out the insides. Then, after the middle is completely dry, trim one hole to be a little larger so you can refill the center of the egg with confetti. Hide these special eggs along with the other eggs for your Easter egg hunt. The lucky finders of these eggs then have the "privilege" of chasing the other children, trying to smash the fragile confetti eggs over the other hunters' heads.

Money Egg

"In our family, there was always one special egg that was hidden in the yard in a particularly difficult place to find. It was the egg that everyone hoped they would recover, as inside it held a 'grand prize' of ten dollars."

—Katie Iverson Baird

Playing the Easter Bunny

Choose some widows or single folks in your neighborhood and play the Easter Bunny to them. Decorate special baskets just for them, including treats and mementos they might enjoy. Leave the basket on the doorstep and ring the doorbell. Stay there if you would like to visit with them, or run away quickly if you prefer to perform this service in secret.

Egg Dying and Decorating

Get together and dye eggs as a family. Have each person do his or her own eggs to be hidden for Easter. Use crayons to create different designs before you dip the eggs in the dye. You can even use feathers, sequins, and beads for added sparkle! Make it a contest for "most creative" or "most colorful" or "best design."

Easter Week Reminders

"Easter Week is an important one for us. We focus on Easter that Sunday through Sunday and do things to help us remember what happened on each particular day. We break a donkey pinata on the Passover Sunday that Christ entered Jerusalem on a donkey, feed the kids Fig Newtons when we talk about how He cursed the fig tree, visit the temple on the day Christ spent all day in the temple teaching, and so forth."

—Sharlene Hawkes

EGG ROLL-OFF

"Saturday evening before Easter we have the Annual Iverson Family Easter Egg Roll-Off. We each pick one or two 'racer' eggs that we will use in the roll-off. Two people line up facing each other, holding their eggs atop opposite sides of a 'half-pipe' ramp made of cardboard. On the count of three, both competitors let go of their eggs, which roll to the center of the curved cardboard, hitting each other. If your egg cracks, you are out of the competition. The race continues until only one egg is left intact. Our family prize is a little stuffed rabbit that gets passed around each year to the winner. The rule is that if you win, you must display the rabbit somewhere in your home for the next year, and then bring it back the following year to pass on to the new winner."

—Katie Iverson Baird

EASTER BONNET PARADE

Have a traditional Easter bonnet parade. Gather around the table together to make your Easter bonnets. You can start with straw hats and decorate those, or begin completely from scratch with paper bags and construction paper. Include extended family for added fun. Parade up and down your street to show off your bonnets to the neighborhood.

Make Your Own Easter Baskets

Work together as a family to make your own Easter baskets. Use old ice-cream containers, dairy cartons, produce baskets, egg cartons, or plastic milk bottles. Accent with feathers, dried pasta, and fabric scraps. Line them up where all Easter visitors can see them.

Scriptural Account of Easter

Take time to gather as a family and read the scriptural account of the Passover and Resurrection. It seems that reading the scriptures has become a popular Christmas event, but it can become a hallowed Easter tradition as well that will strengthen testimony in the Savior and His gospel.

A True Easter Gift

Each year surprise your family members with new pictures of the Savior to put in their rooms or carry in their scriptures. Write your testimony on the back of the pictures to remind them of your faith in the Lord and to strengthen their own testimonies. Hold a special family testimony meeting for all to participate in.

Easter Bunny Early

A few days before Easter, sit down as a family and write a letter to the Easter Bunny requesting that he come to your home on Saturday instead of Easter Sunday, to help you preserve the sacred nature of the Sabbath day.

EASTER CERAMIC

"Each child in our family has an individual Easter ceramic figurine made by Mom when we were all very small. Now, on Easter morning, as we are looking for our Easter baskets, we can identify our own by finding the one that has our personal ceramic."

—Julie Knapp Meyer

Mother's Day

Our family has found true joy and bonded through the celebration of Mother's Day, as we have focused on the lives and contributions of our mothers and grandmothers. It has become a great tradition to also recognize the many "mothers" around us, women with or without children, including sisters, aunts, teachers, and neighbors who have been wonderful examples in our lives.

Paper Favor-Flower Bouquet

Have each member of the family make a flower out of construction paper. Help them come up with a service that they can do for Mom or Grandma. Write the idea down on their own flower, and then put the flowers in a basket or vase to present. Label the bouquet as "favor flowers." Then set aside a day when the entire family can carry out their tasks together.

A Garden for Mom

Spend the Saturday before Mother's Day planting a flower garden. Have each child choose a different flower he or she would like to plant for Mom, and spend the afternoon putting them in the ground as a family.

Children's Photograph

Each May, have a family photograph taken, just of the children, to remind Mother of the joy she has in her children. Choose a particular spot in the home to display the picture. Then, each year on Mother's Day, replace the picture with an updated one.

Mom's Makeover

Take Mom out to the nearest beauty parlor and treat her to a total makeover. Watch as they change her hair, do her makeup, and pamper her all around. Stay close by and chat as she receives a manicure, pedicure, and facial massage.

Pamper Pack

Each year, give Mom a "pamper pack." Every member of the family includes a gift in the package that Mom can use to indulge herself. It may be some lotion, some perfume, or just a good book that Mom can enjoy reading during some relaxation time. Each year she will look forward to getting her pack with which to spoil herself, and the family will enjoy coming up with new ways to help her do so.

Homemade Picture Frame

Make a family picture frame. Each child could do his or her own frame, or the family could all work together on one frame. Fashion a frame for a photo or spend time decorating a mat for a framed family picture. Have each person sign the mat or add a little drawing to show his or her personality. This is a great gift for Grandma to show off to her friends.

Gift of Doing Nothing

Gather the children and assign chores and tasks to give Mom or Grandma a "do nothing" day. Have the children work together to cook meals, clean rooms, and fold laundry. Save a seat in the house where Mom or Grandma can oversee the production while reading from a favorite book or listening to her favorite music.

Poetry

Dig deep into your creative side and write a yearly poem to Mom. Reminisce on your childhood memories, or simply bring back the highlights of the past year. Save the poems in a book to be added to on each Mother's Day.

Breakfast in Bed

Mother's Day is a wonderful time to treat Mom to breakfast in bed. Cook all of her favorites, and don't forget to accent with flowers or greenery. If she would rather, make it simple, with yogurt and fruit, or get elaborate with omelettes and crepes. She will enjoy her meal under the covers no matter what you prepare!

Ladies' Luncheon

"All the females in our extended family eight years of age and older have a special luncheon the day before Mother's Day. We dress in our best and all have a great time being together as mothers and future mothers."

—Kay Cannon

Memorial Day

Observing Memorial Day through the years has given our family a deep appreciation for loved ones who have passed away. It has increased our eternal perspective and given us a greater sense of where each one of us fits into the family circle, and of the legacy passed down that we must continue.

Family Flag

Make an annual family flag to fly outside your home on Memorial Day, in addition to the American flag. Either have each member decorate his or her own section of the flag, or have all help to create a design that typifies the family as a whole. Explain to one another why you include specific designs, and why each design is special to that year. Display all the past flags if you wish to see the changes that have taken place in your family over the years.

Potluck Dinner

Get together for an extended family potluck dinner. Children will love seeing relatives who may not be close enough to visit on a frequent basis. Reminisce about those relatives who have passed away, and teach children about the lives of their ancestors.

Ancestor Trek

"On Memorial Day we always travel with our extended family to all of the places where our ancestors are buried—Meadow, Kanosh, and Ephraim. We start out at 6:30 A.M. with a chuck-wagon breakfast in Meadow, then have a picnic later in the day at Kanosh. We spend an enjoyable day with loved ones, remembering those who have gone on before."

—Susan Walker

Visit the Cemetery

Take time to visit a cemetery as a family. Pick special grave sites to visit, or walk around discovering others. Read what the families of the departed have written on their stones. Talk about what you as a family would like others to say about you once you have departed, and discuss the legacy you would like to pass on to your family upon your death.

Family History Library

Visit a Family History Library in your area. Take a tour, and learn how to use the sources available to research and find the members of your family. Discover your heritage and the blood lines from which you came. You may even find someone "famous" to whom you are related. Discuss the importance of ancestry with your children to give them a sense of belonging within your own family.

Take a Hike

"A Memorial Day tradition for our family is to go hiking to Grandeur Peak in Salt Lake City, Utah, and then eat snacks and treats when we get to the top."

—Nancy McMurray

Fourth of July

Celebrating the nation's birthday is of great importance in our family. We feel it's essential to instill
in family members a love and loyalty and respect
for our country and its leaders. This respect has fil-
tered into other aspects of our lives and helped us
maintain a healthy and supportive view of our
nation.

When You Wish Upon a Star

Because the star is such an important symbol on our flag, representing the individual states that make up our country, the Fourth of July is a good time to lie down on blankets outside as a family and look up at the stars in the sky. Have each person express a wish for the country and for the family as they "wish upon a star."

Family T-Shirts

"Pull out the permanent markers, puffy paints, and fabric crayons, and have members of the family make their own patriotic T-shirts. Before beginning, explain to the younger children the purpose for the colors in the American flag, and the importance of each symbol of the stars and stripes. Have them use these symbols and colors when creating their own shirts. Be sure to date each shirt and mark names, as they will become treasures in the years to come."

—Marilyn Hales

Neighborhood Parade

Gather the family and neighbors who would like to participate and have a parade. Decorate bikes, strollers, wagons, and wheelbarrows with crepe paper, balloons, and streamers. Wear hats, and be sure to include red, white, and blue somewhere in your outfit. Have some traditional patriotic music accompany you as you march up and down the street.

AMERICA'S BIRTHDAY CARDS

Make and decorate birthday cards to America. Display the cards all month long where family and friends can see them, and reminisce about the importance of our country's founding.

A STAR-SPANGLED DISCUSSION

Read aloud the words to the national anthem, "The Star-Spangled Banner." Sometimes words get lost in the music and can have more meaning when read straight. Discuss the circumstances under which the anthem was written, who Francis Scott Key was, and his other contributions to our country.

MEMORIZE POETRY

Learn and recite poetry specific to the patriotic holiday. Have the family learn "Paul Revere's Ride" or the Preamble to the Constitution of the United States. Invite extended family members over and make the recitation part of the evening's celebration.

VENERATE A VETERAN

Invite a veteran to your home on the Fourth of July, and have a special devotional on patriotism. Sing patriotic songs, and then have the guest speaker share his or her special feelings about America and the joys of living in our country. Begin and end with a prayer of gratitude for the freedoms we enjoy.

FAMILY CAMPING

Go camping or hiking to enjoy the beauties of the country. Visit a national park or monument where possible. Teach the children the importance of recognizing the blessing of living in such a beautiful country. Point out things that may be unique to our country, or even to your geographic region. Talk about the different climates across the country, and about the "melting pot" phenomenon of America, with so many different races of people living here.

BIRTHDAY PARTY AND GIFTS

Have a birthday party for America. Serve birthday cake and ice cream and sing "Happy Birthday." As a family, write down specific "gifts" you might give to America that will make you better citizens or will make the country a better place for all those around you. Include ideas for beautifying the neighborhood or treating others with respect.

AFTERNOON AND EVENING AT THE PARK

Go as a family to enjoy a community fireworks show. Take a picnic dinner and enjoy the day playing games, throwing a Frisbee, napping on a blanket, reading, and enjoying snacks during the daylight hours before night falls and the fireworks begin.

Rise and Shine!

On the Fourth of July, wake up the family with "The Star-Spangled Banner" resonating throughout your home.

Patriotic Barbecue

Along with the regular barbecue items, serve side dishes that are red, white, and blue, including strawberries, raspberries, watermelon, blueberries, red or blue punch, ambrosia salad with whipped cream, macaroni salad with mayonnaise, and red gelatin salad decorated with whipped cream and blueberries to resemble the American Flag. Serve patriotic ice cream for dessert.

Clothes for the Country

Have every family member dress in red, white, and blue, to show their patriotism. Buy special socks, ribbons, and hats to add to the occasion.

Pioneer Day

Different pioneer activities have given our family an appreciation for the great struggles and trials the pioneers suffered. This is an especially good time to help our children understand the tremendous sacrifices our forebears made so that we can worship and live as we do.

Pioneer Dress

Dress up like pioneers and have a pioneer breakfast together. Eat mush and fried potatoes, flapjacks and bacon. Warm hot cocoa over a fire, and toast your bread the old-fashioned way over the flames.

A Day in the Life of a Pioneer

Spend an entire day without using any modern conveniences. Turn off the television, don't use the telephone, and walk everywhere you go. Sleep outside in the backyard as a family with blankets. Wash your hair in a tub of water, make butter together, and do some wash by hand. That evening, talk about the blessings of living during this modern time, and the things you feel you could live without.

Farming Day

Go for a horseback ride or a hayride at a farm. Take time to learn about how the animals are used to get the work done around the farm. Perhaps you might even milk a cow and enjoy the fresh cream and milk.

Church History Sites

Where possible, visit a Church history site and learn something about the pioneers. Travel to a different site each year, or make an annual trek to the same site and refresh your memory about things you might have forgotten.

Pioneer Museum

Visit a pioneer museum. See the different inventions they used, and explain how those devices have developed into tools we use today. Examine the beautiful handiwork used in making the quilts and wall hangings on display. Look at the different toys the pioneer children had to keep them entertained, and compare them to the toys children have today.

Dutch-Oven Dinner

For dinner, cook in a Dutch oven. You could go into a canyon or a nearby park, or simply cook in your own backyard. Find a pioneer recipe and make it for your family. Have each family member help prepare the dinner, heat the coals, and cook the meal.

Handiwork

Each year, work as a family on a handicraft project. Work on a quilt, or try hand-stitching some hems on clothes or towels. Find someone who can teach you to knit or crochet, and have family members make their own items to pass on to their families someday.

Taffy Pull

Get a traditional taffy recipe and pull taffy together as a family, just like the pioneers did. Have fun twisting the taffy into your own original designs; then enjoy eating it together.

Neighborhood Square Dance

Have a square dance with some neighbors. Involve extended family and friends to cook up some traditional pioneer desserts to serve as refreshments, like pies and cakes. Make sure to wear your pioneer dresses and hats, and, if possible, dance to live fiddles!

Cemetery Tour

Take a tour of a cemetery near you and find headstones of those who lived in the pioneer days. Read about the pioneers, especially about your own ancestors who might have been pioneers. Talk about the legacy the pioneers gave to us and the traits that we will pass on to our families, such as faith, hard work, and perseverance.

Sleep Under the Stars

"On the 24th of July, we always sleep out in our yard the night before, and get up early and go to the canyon to eat breakfast."

—Nellee Woodland

Pioneer Walk

"Every summer we go on a long walk. Each time we come to an intersection, we flip a coin. If it comes up heads, we turn right; if it comes up tails, we turn left. At the end of the walk, we have refreshing snacks."

—Kay Cannon

Back to School

We have tried to make returning to school as memorable and fun as possible every year. We have stressed the importance of education so that the end of the summer marks the beginning of something new and exciting. Now, our children actually look forward to going back to school, meeting new friends, and having new experiences.

Back-to-School Sleep-Over

Invite extended family members to an overnight back-to-school party the weekend before school starts. Include lots of lunch-box-style treats for them to snack on, or decorate a special cake to look like an apple, a ruler, or a sheet of notebook paper. Tuck little notes or trinkets under their pillows before they go to sleep to get them excited about their return to school. You might even have them practice waking up to an alarm clock, now that summer vacation is coming to an end.

Sing Your Way to School

Use the drive time in the car on the way to school as a way to learn some new songs in harmony. Even if the school is only ten minutes away, the drive can be great fun when all siblings are singing at the tops of their lungs in two-part or even three-part harmony. Getting everyone out the door can be chaotic, and this singing time restores good spirits!

New School Supplies Surprise

Each year, as your family prepares to go back to a school and work routine, surprise each family member with a new backpack or briefcase to carry everything in. Fill it full of pencils, pens, paper, folders, and anything else they might need for the upcoming year. Don't forget to include their favorite snacks and treats to make your surprise even sweeter.

Back-to-School Shopping

Do all of your back-to-school shopping together as a family. Malls are great for this, as they have stores to fit every style. Wait for each other while trying on clothes, or break up into pairs and meet at a designated time for lunch. For a variation, have each child take a turn going shopping alone with Mom or Dad, enjoying some private time together to talk about the upcoming year.

Good Grade Reward

"In my family, whenever someone got straight A's, they got to choose where the entire family would go out to dinner. We all tried to do our best in school, and this way we were all rewarded, but straight A's got the greater reward."

—Elizabeth Larson

Graduation Trip

"We have made it a tradition in our family to take a family trip whenever one of our children graduates from high school or college. We have been to Boston, New York, Washington, D.C., Hawaii, Mexico, and California."

—Marion Clark

Displayed Portraits

Every year, as the new school pictures come out, hang them in a prominent place in the home where every person senses his or her place and importance in the family.

STRAIGHT-A DINNER

When a child gets straight A's on his or her report card, surprise the family with a Straight-A Dinner. Cook a dinner with a menu full of "A" foods, such as Asian stir fry, almond chicken, asparagus, ambrosia salad, and apple pie.

LUNCH LOVE NOTES

Use your children's lunch boxes and backpacks as teaching tools. Include quotes and little notes of encouragement on their napkins or other papers. They will look forward each day to the words of wisdom and love from Mom or Dad while they are away from home for a few hours.

AFTER-SCHOOL SNACKS

"Every day after school, we all got excited as our car pulled into the driveway, knowing that there was a treat waiting on the counter for us. Every day, Mom had neatly lined up snacks: raisins, apples, granola bars, and drinks. We really looked forward to seeing what awaited us on the kitchen counter."

—Tiffany L. Johnson

FAMILY BUDGET

Sit down as a family and make a budget for the coming school year. Include ideas for allowance, as well as planning ahead for the upcoming summer vacation. Give each person the responsibility of proposing a plan for earning money, including a way to work together to save enough for something the whole family can enjoy.

EDUCATION WEEK

Attend Campus Education Week at the BYU-Hawaii, BYU-Idaho, or BYU-Provo campus. Attend classes together or split up and take good notes that you can share later that evening. Talk as a family about the many things you have learned, and discuss ways you can incorporate your new ideas into the upcoming months.

FATHER'S BLESSINGS

Gather as a family for father's blessings before the new school year. The blessings can be given in private alone with Mom and Dad, or as a family where all family members can participate and hear one another's blessings. Either way, each person will share in the Spirit and increase in testimony of the power of the priesthood.

FAMILY PLANNING

Every year before school starts, have a big "family summit" meeting with all family members to plan scripture study times for the upcoming year, family home evenings, chore distribution, and family prayer times. Plan out the entire year as far as possible, so that all family members are involved in each other's lives.

Labor Day

Some of the happiest times we share are when we are working together as a family. As we work, we talk, laugh, and sing, and when the work is done, not only have we accomplished a task but we have bonded in the process.

Funny Vegetables

To help celebrate the new harvest, have a funny vegetable search. Go either to your own garden or to a nearby market and scout out some of the misshapen vegetables and fruit from the crops. Go home and eat the funny shapes, or try dressing them up to make them even stranger and more bizarre.

Neighborhood Cleanup

Participate as a family in beautifying a part of your neighborhood. Help some neighbors do their yard work, or clean out gutters around your home. Perhaps you could go to a community park and pick up trash or pull weeds together. Maybe you could even adopt a section of the local highway by contacting your local officials, and take responsibility for keeping it clean.

Clean All Day, Party All Night

Spend the whole morning cleaning the house, getting things ready for the upcoming winter weather. Clean out the flower beds, fix up the yard, and organize the home inside from top to bottom. Then, after a long day of work, reward yourselves with an all-night party. Go out to dinner, go bowling, or just sit and watch a video. Eat ice cream and relax in your newly polished surroundings.

Fall "Spring-Cleaning"

As a family, go through the garage, attic, or bedroom closets and fill one bag together that you can take to a local charity or thrift store. Decide the things that you can part with in order to improve a less-fortunate family's life.

Harvest Dinner

Reap the rewards of the harvest in your own yard. As a family, pick the vegetables and fruits from your family garden. Have a special dinner together eating only those things that came from your garden. This helps everyone truly appreciate the payoff of cultivating a garden.

Halloween

There's something exciting and even liberating about dressing up, playing games, and eating sweets on this favorite holiday! When we celebrate the time as a family, we learn that sharing that fun and excitement brings us closer together. It's a perfect time to create memories!

NEIGHBORHOOD PHANTOM

Start the "neighborhood phantom" during the first week of October. "Strike" three different neighbors' homes, leaving a treat and a note at their doorstep telling them they have been "hit" by the Halloween phantom. Instruct them to do the same to two other neighbors, or the spirit of the phantom will haunt them for the entire month of October. They must then place a note on their door saying they have already been hit. As the "phantom" continues to strike around the neighborhood, see how quickly the spirit of giving spreads.

ANNUAL CATTAIL ROAST

"We host a neighborhood 'cattail roast' and invite all the neighbors to join us in our driveway for hot dogs. We get a large oil drum to hold the fire over which we can roast hot dogs, and neighbors bring different side dishes, drinks, and desserts to share. As dinner comes to an end, the trick-or-treaters may then set out on full stomachs!"

—Tom and Kaye Swallow

PUMPKIN CARVING AND SEED EATING

"Every year as a family, we each choose pumpkins and everyone gathers at Mom's to carve them. After cleaning out the seeds, we bake them for eating. When the carving is completed, we light each pumpkin and take our annual picture of our creations."

—Michael Dustin

TRUNK OR TREAT

Gather the neighborhood together for a "trunk or treat." Have all the neighbors bring their cars to a designated parking lot decorated with Halloween ghosts, pumpkins, and spider webs. Distribute treats to the neighborhood children from the trunks of your cars. It makes for safer trick-or-treating in a more controlled environment.

HALLOWEEN SERVICE

In the days before Halloween, go "serve-or-treating" around the neighborhood. At each home, ask if you may come in and perform a service. Change lightbulbs, vacuum, rake leaves, or do dishes. After your service is complete, leave them with a little Halloween treat.

PUMPKIN PATCH

Grow your own pumpkins for Halloween. Have the family members scratch designs and pictures into their own individual pumpkins while they are small, and watch the creations change and grow along with the pumpkins.

MATCHING COSTUMES

Trick-or-treat as a family in matching costumes. Have family members go as different colored crayons, or as different kinds of animals. Get creative and enjoy spending this holiday as a family.

Apple Witch Carving

At the first of October, buy an apple for each member of your family. Have each person peel his or her apple and carve a face into it. Dangle the fresh apples from strings and, throughout the month, watch the apples turn into wrinkled, browned, witch faces! They make great Halloween ornaments, and each person can participate in the decorating.

Family Day Halloween

"On Halloween night, we invite a neighbor family to dinner and always have the same menu: chili in a hollowed-out pumpkin, pomegranate and apple salad, carrots and celery sticks, scones with butter and honey, and hot wassail to drink. All the children go trick-or-treating with the fathers while the mothers stay home and answer the doors."

—Jeanne English

Witch's Dinner

Purchase plain black witch hats for every member of the family, along with beads, silk flowers, fabric squares, and other craft items for family members to use to decorate their hats to their own personalities. Then, have a dinner complete with a menu of "witchy" items. You could have "frog-eye salad," "sand-witches," and "dragon scale" chips. Get creative!

CARAMEL APPLES

"After the children return from trick-or-treating on Halloween, we always enjoy fixing and eating caramel apples."

—Vera Nielsen

DINNER IN A PUMPKIN

"We have a favorite hamburger, rice, and water-chestnut recipe that we stick in a big pumpkin (with a face colored on it) and bake in the oven for an hour or so. We have this for dinner every Halloween before going out trick-or-treating."

—Sharlene Hawkes

PUMPKIN CAROLING

"Go pumpkin caroling! We wrote Halloween lyrics to some of our favorite Christmas carols, then delivered decorated pumpkins to our elderly and widowed neighbors and caroled to them."

—Colleen Peterson

TRICKS FOR TREATS

"My husband, Dean, loves Halloween. He always encourages the trick-or-treaters to come inside the house and perform for him by singing a song, saying a poem, or turning a somersault. After this they are rewarded with a treat."

—Marion Clark

HAUNTED GINGERBREAD HOUSES

Rather than reserve gingerbread houses for Christmas, try making haunted houses instead! Use chocolate frosting instead of white frosting to create a "haunted" look. Be sure to have plenty of candy corn, gumdrops, and orange sprinkles on hand before you begin!

TRADITIONAL TREAT

"At the Neerings home, we always make homemade spudnuts for the trick-or-treaters. Our grandma always comes to the house to help glaze the 120 spudnuts we make."

—Colleen Neerings

Veterans Day

This holiday is an appropriate time to honor those men and women who have served our country to preserve our freedom. We can learn much from the experiences of these selfless people, and commemorating their efforts in thoughtful ways gives us a greater appreciation for their sacrifices on our behalf.

AIRCRAFT-CARRIER COOKIE

"My father served on an aircraft carrier in World War II. One year, my wife and I made a giant cookie in the shape of an aircraft carrier and decorated it with gray frosting to make it look exactly like Dad's ship. We then accented the large cookie with smaller cookies in the shapes of stars and airplanes. We took it to him, and each member of our family expressed our gratitude to him for his service to give us the freedoms we enjoy."

—John Bytheway

CHURCH MOVIE

Watch the video *Saints at War.* This BYU production highlights the lives of many faithful World War II veterans who had miraculous experiences while serving our country. Share testimonies together as a family, and then have a special family prayer expressing gratitude for those men and women who fought so hard for us.

VISIT A VETERAN

Arrange to spend time listening to a veteran's stories about his or her war experiences. Come prepared with questions to ask to help direct the conversation. Leave a small thank-you gift or treat with the person. After leaving, write thank-you notes to the veteran, mentioning specific things that you enjoyed learning about when you visited.

War Movie

Rent and watch a war movie. There are hundreds available that would be age-appropriate for your family's specific needs. Talk afterward about the freedoms we enjoy, and have each person express his or her feelings of gratitude for living in our country and for the people who have helped to maintain our freedoms.

Airplane Flying Contest

Make and decorate paper airplanes and have a flying contest. Include prizes for the most creatively decorated as well as the most aerodynamic. Books are available if you need help in paper-airplane design. This is fun for all age groups.

Patriotic Caroling

Go "country caroling." Sing your favorite patriotic songs, and target the homes of veterans who might live in your area. Dress for the occasion, with soldiers' costumes, or simply in the colors of the country's flag.

War in the Scriptures

Take time to read through some of the "war chapters" in the book of Alma (try Alma 43–62). Teach the family about why there are wars, and why we believe in fighting for good causes. Talk about the wickedness that led to certain wars, and the righteousness that allowed the victors to prevail.

Boat Races

Have a paper boat race. Let each person make a boat out of paper, including sails or propellers. Blow through straws for "wind" and see whose boat can cross the finish line first. For a variation, make propellers using the spring action from a wound rubber band to propel the boats in competition.

Veteran Remembrance

Take the family to any local services that might be held in honor of veterans. These may include a flag ceremony, a devotional, or a parade.

Thanksgiving

No matter where we spend this holiday, we have learned the importance of spending it as a family. We take time to reflect on our blessings and express love and gratitude for each other. It has become an especially meaningful time for us to realize all of our blessings.

Alphabetical Blessings

Before dinner, play "alphabetical gratitude." Go around the table and have each person say something he or she is grateful for. The first person names something that starts with the letter *a,* and the next person names something beginning with the letter *b.* Continue around the table as many times as necessary until the entire alphabet is complete.

Count Your Many Rice Kernels

While setting the table, hide a few rice kernels underneath each of the plates. As you are seated for dinner, have the unsuspecting diners look underneath their plates and count the number of rice kernels. Starting at the head of the table, go around and have each person name a blessing for each rice kernel found beneath his or her plate.

Pilgrim Record Reading

Find a historical account of the first Thanksgiving. Read it together with the family on the night before Thanksgiving. Talk about why we continue to celebrate Thanksgiving, and what practices the Pilgrims established that we still follow today. Research and find any ancestors you can who lived at the time of the first Thanksgiving dinner, and include them in your discussion.

Thanksgiving Greetings

Send out Thanksgiving cards to your friends and relatives. Include the many things you are grateful for, including the specific blessings you have enjoyed that year. It will be a nice surprise for those who are not expecting a card for this season.

Family Football Game

Have an annual "Turkey Bowl." Include extended family, and gather together for a giant football game. This may include men, women, boys, and girls, or it might be a nice way for the "boys" to pass the time while the women complete the finishing touches right before dinner.

Neighborhood Pie Delivery

Bake pumpkin pies, or other seasonal favorites, and deliver them to your neighbors. Work together in the kitchen as a family, assigning out each step of the pie to a different family member. Go as a family to deliver the treats, to see the gratitude that service brings.

In Pilgrim Fashion

Spend a little bit of time before Thanksgiving dinner making Pilgrim hats as a family. If you have extended family members joining you for dinner, make hats for them as well. Wear the hats during dinner to remind you of the first Thanksgiving dinner the Pilgrims held.

PLACE-CARD ORNAMENTS

Make personalized wooden place cards for your dinner guests to take home and hang on their Christmas trees the following season. Be sure to date each ornament as the years pass, and then each Christmas you can reminisce about Thanksgivings past as you decorate your tree.

FESTIVE NUT CUPS

Have the family get together to make *Mayflower* nut cups for dinner commemorating the Pilgrims' ship. Use construction paper, and let the children get creative with their own boats. Fill the cups with autumn-colored goodies, including nuts and orange, yellow, brown, and red candies.

BEST DRESSED

Every year, make Thanksgiving a more reverent event by having all of the family dress in Sunday best for dinner. Treat the day with respect, as if it were a Sunday or other sacred day.

PERSONAL GRATITUDE PRAYER

On the night before Thanksgiving, have each member of the family retreat to a private part of the home for an individual prayer of gratitude. Instruct each person to thank Heavenly Father for his or her specific blessings without asking for anything.

Volunteer at a Shelter

Share your blessings with others. Volunteer as a family at a local shelter, serving food to the homeless. Help prepare the food that will be served, then stay after to dine with some of the less fortunate partakers of the dinner.

Turkey for Dessert

After dinner, have each family member make an apple-and-gumdrop turkey. Get toothpicks to stack the gumdrops on for tail feathers, and poke them into the apple, which is the body of the turkey. Make a head out of construction paper. Be sure to admire each person's creativity.

Animal Thanksgiving

Prepare a feast for the birds by spreading pine cones with peanut butter and then rolling them in bird seed or peanuts. Tie these tasty morsels on the trees in your yard with red yarn. It is fun to watch the birds eat their own feast.

Fast and Feast

Come to Thanksgiving dinner after fasting for twenty-four hours. Spend that time focused on the many blessings you have been given, as well as on coming closer to the Spirit. After the fast, gather as a family for a testimony meeting, sharing your convictions about the gospel. After the testimonies, feast on a traditional Thanksgiving dinner!

GOING WITHOUT

Play the gratitude game. Make a list of about ten "modern" items that we all enjoy, such things as the microwave, the car, the television, the radio, the refrigerator, the computer, and the dryer. Then, have each person go down the list and name three things that they think they could live without. This should help all of us realize how much we take for granted the things that our forebears lived without.

GRATITUDE TREE

Have paper leaves cut out and laid on a table with a marker. As guests arrive for Thanksgiving, have them write down a few things they are grateful for on the paper leaves, and hang them on a bare branch that you have potted like a tree. Later, read the leaves that everyone has put on the tree to help each other remember the many blessings we all enjoy.

TABLECLOTH REMINDER

Create a "thanks" tablecloth. Set a permanent marker at each place setting, and have the dinner guests write down the things that they are most thankful for on the tablecloth underneath their plates. Each year, set the table with the same tablecloth, with new markers, and have the guests again write down their blessings on a blank spot on the cloth.

Thanksgiving Surprise

The night before Thanksgiving, share your blessings of abundance with friends and neighbors. Surprise them with a note of gratitude for knowing them, along with a special gift of your own choosing. Leave it on their doorstep for them to see on Thanksgiving morning.

Appreciation Pockets

Make a special poster with a pocket for each member of the family. Provide slips of paper on which family members can write down the things that they are grateful for throughout the month of November. On Thanksgiving morning, read the papers and remember your blessings together.

Dinner and a Movie

"We love to go to movies on Thanksgiving night. It is a great way to relax after cleaning up from the big dinner, and to spend time seeing some of the new holiday releases."

—Christian Meyer

Christmas Shopping Head Start

As so many stores have their greatest sales on the day after Thanksgiving, sleep over at someone's home Thanksgiving night, and then wake up together bright and early for the special store openings. It is amazing how many other people are ready that early to rush in and get their bargains!

BREAKFAST SOLUTION

"To solve the problem of whether to spend Thanksgiving at my family's home or my husband's family's home, we have the perfect solution. Every Thanksgiving morning we go to his parents' home for a big Thanksgiving breakfast. Then, later in the day, we go to my parents' home and enjoy a traditional Thanksgiving dinner."

—Cathy Burbidge

TURKEY BOWLING

"Every Thanksgiving morning we have our annual turkey bowl. This means that we all go bowling together. We have a traveling trophy that goes to the bowler with the highest score. We find the bowling alley is not very crowded at this time and the whole family can have a great time."

—Ada Coleman

PASSING THE LIGHT

Set the table with a candle at each person's plate. Starting at the head of the table, have the person light his or her candle, expressing gratitude for several things. Then, that person holds out the candle to the next person to light his or her own candle from while giving thanks for blessings. Continue on until the entire table is lit with everyone's "gratitude light."

ANNUAL PIE PIG-OUT

"Because Thanksgiving dinner can be such a filling meal, we have dessert the night before. We each bring one pie, and my son makes several special ones. We make sure that each person's favorite pie is represented, and that we all get as much pie as we want, without having to save room from dinner."

—Michele Staker

Christmas Season

The birth of the Savior is such a monumental event that the entire month of December can be filled with celebration. Try extending the Christmas season with traditions sprinkled all throughout the month, taking as many opportunities as possible to gather together, to enjoy one another, and to revel in the joy and gladness of the holiday.

$\mathcal{T}$WELVE DAYS OF CHRISTMAS

For the twelve days leading up to Christmas, beginning on December 13, leave a secret gift and a poem every night at the doorstep of an unsuspecting family or widow. On the first night, leave one item; the second night, two; the third night, three, and so on. Some suggestions might include: one poinsettia, two loaves of banana bread, three candles, four gingerbread men, five ornaments, six popcorn balls, seven Christmas stories, eight pieces of fruit, nine candy bars, ten hot chocolate packets, eleven candy canes, and twelve sweet rolls. Each poem should begin with "On the _____ day of Christmas . . ." For example:

> On the eighth day of Christmas,
> We bring the Harvest's bounty:
> A basket filled with luscious fruit
> From farmers in the county.

On the last night (usually Christmas Eve), the poem included with the gift reveals the name of your family. We include this special poem:

> These days of Christmas have brought joy
> To us as we have given.
> We also hope your heart's been touched,
> And felt a bit of heaven.
> And just in case you're wondering
> Why we have done this thing:
> This time of year turns many souls
> To Christ our Lord and King.

For His example has been set;
We feel it through and through.
He showed great love to everyone;
Now we give love to you.
Love from the Loveridge Family

We like to fold the bottom of the paper and tape it up to hide our name, so the family will take the time to read the poem, and not just skip to the end to discover our identity.

After you leave the last gift at the doorstep, run and hide as usual. Wait a few minutes, and then return to the front door, caroling. Many secret acts of service are done throughout the year, but this becomes a great teaching moment. Your children will see the love and deep gratitude on the faces of those whom they have served, and they will always remember that special moment when they were able to hear firsthand the expressions of joy for the service they gave.

Secret Santa

Early in the month of December, write down all of the family members' names on individual pieces of paper, and then have each person draw out one of the names. Each person does secret acts of service every day for the person drawn. On Christmas Day, each member of the family reveals who he or she has served all month long by giving a Christmas present to that person. This activity will create a great spirit of love and giving in the home for the days preceding the great Christmas celebration.

Fun with Gingerbread

Have guests bring one or two of their favorite treats to help decorate gingerbread houses, or even gingerbread trains, and get to work! Graham crackers can be substituted for gingerbread for ease and convenience. Let everyone make his or her own creation, or work together for a masterpiece. Create your own little Christmas village from the results, or give them away to neighbors and friends. Royal icing (recipe below) dries hard to hold the candy in place.

Royal Icing:
2 egg whites
1 teaspoon cream of tartar
2 cups powdered sugar

Whip egg whites with cream of tartar until stiff peaks form. Slowly add powdered sugar and beat until stiff. Use immediately to assemble walls of gingerbread house and to keep decorations in place, or cover bowl with a wet towel to keep the icing from hardening until you are ready to use it.

Activity Basket

Write a list of fun activities to do during the holidays, and put them on individual slips of paper. Ideas might include going ice skating, decorating the tree, baking cookies, or visiting friends. Each night in December, draw out one slip of paper to dictate the evening's activities.

CHRISTMAS AROUND THE WORLD

For each week in the month of December, have a special family home evening highlighting a different country and its traditions surrounding Christmas. Complete the lesson with food and desserts from the country chosen. The family will have a greater appreciation for the birth of the Savior and for the sacredness of the holiday worldwide.

CHRISTMAS CALENDAR

Buy or make a traditional advent calendar for the days before Christmas. Each calendar day could have a new ornament to be hung on the tree, or a small treat for the family to enjoy.

CHRISTMAS DAILY SERVICE

Create a family "service" advent calendar. Each day, have someone pull out a prepared slip of paper with some service that you can do together as a family. You might serve a neighbor, or perhaps keep the service in the home by helping out one another. Performing a service each day will truly help to bring about the true spirit of Christmas.

BEDTIME CAROLS AND STORIES

For the month of December, have a Christmas theme at bedtime. Sing Christmas songs, and read from 3 Nephi and Luke about the first Christmas. Find special books and stories dedicated to Christmas themes and ideas.

See the Painted Town

Find a night during the Christmas season when you can all pile in the car to tour the homes and businesses that are decorated with Christmas lights.

Picture Ornaments

At Christmas, sit down with the family and have everyone create their own ornaments with photographs of themselves on them. As the tree has become a central figure in Christmas decorating, it will show that the central focus of the family is each other.

Binding Memories

"Each Christmas, every family member contributes a written memory from the previous year. We make copies for them to put in their own binders from year to year. One of the greatest joys we have as a family comes when we reflect on the poignant moments of the other family members. As our family has grown, the grandchildren even enjoy adding their own memories to our books."

—Jeanette Grace Zarkou Hamilton

Children's Trees

Give each child his or her own small tree to decorate. Allow them to use their own personalities to choose their colors and decorations. Supply plenty of paper, scissors, glue, glitter, beads, and other craft items for the decorating event.

DIRECTIONAL GIFTS

Have a "left-right" gift exchange. Write a story with a Christmas theme, with as many inclusions of the words *left* and *right* as you can think of. Each person shows up to the party with a present, and all sit in a circle as a narrator begins the story. Each time the guests hear *left* or *right* they are to pass the presents in their laps in that direction. Afterward, open all the gifts to reveal the surprises. For a variation, read "'Twas the Night Before Christmas," and every time the words *a* and *the* are heard, everyone passes his or her gift to the right.

WHITE ELEPHANT GIFT EXCHANGE

Wrap gag gifts, or bring small, inexpensive items, and put them in the center of the room. Draw numbers to determine the order of recipients. The first person chooses a gift from the pile and opens it. The next person may either choose a new gift from the pile or steal the gift from the first person, who must then choose a new gift from the pile. Go through the numerical order until all gifts are opened and everyone has a present.

SUB FOR SANTA

Talk to your bishop or a local schoolteacher to find a family in need of your assistance. Learn of the ages of the children in the family, and shop together for gifts and groceries to help the family enjoy a better Christmas.

Baking Day

Have a family "cookie and goodie" day. Invite all extended family members who can attend to join you as you bake, cook, and concoct delicious treats to be delivered to friends and neighbors.

Elves Among Us

Enlist one of Santa's elves to live at your home in the days before Christmas. Have him leave little personal items around the house to remind the children that he is always taking notes for Santa. Give him a bed to sleep in (one that somehow never gets made in the morning after he awakens), and watch as the family members remain on their best behavior!

Christmas Vacation

Christmas is a wonderful time to take a vacation as a family, particularly if you have no extended family nearby. The family agrees to spend the "Christmas budget" on something they can enjoy together: a trip. The memories and good times will be the greatest present they receive every year.

The Clauses Go to the Hospital

Dress the family as Santa and his elves, or as the "Claus family." Visit a hospital and spread cheer to those who must spend their holiday away from home. Sing and deliver presents and goodwill.

LUMBERJACK'S TREE

Get a permit and go to a forested area near your home to cut down your own family Christmas tree. For those who love to have real trees without the nursery prices, these "do it yourself" chopped trees give special meaning to the event.

CHRISTMAS SYMBOLS

As the family gathers to decorate the home for Christmas, explain to everyone the meaning behind the symbols of Christmas. For example, the green of the tree represents life, the red ornaments the blood of the crucified Lord, the candy cane the crooked staff of the shepherds, the stars the Bethlehem star marking the Savior's birthplace, the candle the "light of the world," and the wreath symbolizes the eternal round of everlasting life that the Savior gave us.

A STOCKING FOR JESUS

Hang a stocking for Jesus on the mantel, and fill it with notes listing all the good things that the family members commit to do to better themselves and those around them.

OLD-FASHIONED SLEIGH RIDE

Wherever possible, take a traditional horse-drawn sleigh ride. Be sure to bring along your singing voices to add to the spirit of the special occasion.

FAMILY PICTURE TREE

Decorate two different trees. Enjoy one traditional tree, complete with presents underneath, but have another, smaller tree with pictures of every family member under it as a reminder to all that the family is the greatest gift.

CHRISTMAS BOOK

"Right after Thanksgiving dinner we all head to the living room, and I bring in a book beautifully wrapped in Christmas paper. The children take turns each year opening it. It is a Christmas book to welcome in the Christmas season. We read one of our Christmas books every day until Christmas Eve, when we read from the most important book of all, the scriptures."

—Barry and Lucie Gibbons

ADVENT CANDLE

"One of our favorite new traditions is the use of a Christmas advent candle, marked into twenty-five segments. Beginning on the first of December, the candle is lit and burned down to the first mark, then blown out. While the candle is burning, we read scriptures pertaining to Christ. After the candle is blown out, we have family prayer. By doing this every day before Christmas, our family keeps the holiday in its proper perspective."

—Elaine Woodruff

CHRISTMAS PUZZLE

"During the Christmas holidays, to keep the children home more and to motivate their friends to visit, we always put up a large jigsaw puzzle—a simple one when the children were small, and more difficult ones as they became older. Sometimes the holidays were nearly over before the puzzle was finished, but it created a real sense of family togetherness as well as happy memories."

—Emily Tyler

DECORATE AS A FAMILY

"Our extended family all gets together for a 'family decorating night' at my parents' home. We each bring one plate of hors d'oeuvres to share, and we spend the evening helping Mom and Dad put up their lights, garlands, and tree. It is a fun way for us all to feel the spirit of the special season."

—Rebekah Perkins Crawford

THE FAMILY TREE

"Our family has a favorite tree-decorating tradition. Every person in our family has a special ornament with his or her name on it, and we all help decorate the tree by hanging our own ornaments. When children or grandchildren are born, or when someone gets married, the new member of the family receives his or her own ornament to hang on the family tree."

—Julie Knapp Meyer

Tangible Gift for Jesus

"Each year you can buy a gift for Jesus from your family. The children can work to earn money for a gift. Gift suggestions might include a new book for the ward library or toys for the ward nursery."

—Marion Clark

Choir Concerts

"Every year, our family goes to hear the Mormon Tabernacle Choir Christmas program. It has become one of my favorite concerts for the entire year, and we love to hear the praises sung to the Savior as we celebrate the day of his birth."

—Tiffany L. Johnson

Grandparents' Treat

"My parents take all their children and grandchildren to a Christmas play somewhere in town following the eating of sack lunches in their home."

—Kay Cannon

Straw for His Manger

"At Christmastime, we have our small porcelain baby Jesus in his swaddling clothes lying in his manger. When anyone in the family does a good deed for another family member, we add a piece of straw to his manger."

—Ruth Egan

Christmas Eve

As we look forward to Christmas, many people count down the days until December 25. However, the celebration on Christmas Eve can be just as important as the festivities on Christmas Day. The memories we create on Christmas Eve are a large part of the fond feelings we have about Christmas-time.

$\mathcal{A}$NNUAL SCRIPTURE READING

Read from Luke 2 in the Bible, and have family members reenact the nativity scene complete with costumes, a manger, and possibly even a stable. Accent with special Christmas music in the background, including "Away in a Manger" and "Silent Night."

$\mathcal{C}$OMING-OF-AGE DINNER

When a young woman in the extended family reaches the age of sixteen, have her join in the tradition of preparing a special dish for a Christmas Eve dinner. As all the family women come together to create the meal, it will be exciting to see what each woman contributes.

$\mathcal{T}$ELL ME THE STORIES OF JESUS

Have each member of the family share his or her favorite story about the Savior and His life and accomplishments. With every family member participating, many aspects of the Savior's ministry and life will be covered. The evening will truly highlight the real reason for the season.

$\mathcal{T}$ALENT NIGHT

Have a family talent night with extended family members on Christmas Eve. Use this time to showcase everyone's musical, artistic, or physical achievements from the previous year.

CHRISTMAS EVE JAMMIES

Hold out one special present to be opened on Christmas Eve. This could be pajamas or new slippers, or a new blanket to be slept with in anticipation of the holiday ahead. Or you might outfit every family member with a new pair of Christmas socks!

KIDS SLEEP TOGETHER

Having all of the children in the family sleep together in the same room is a great way for the children to share the excitement and anticipation of Christmas together. This might ensure that they will all wake up together, so that Christmas morning will begin with everyone ready at the same time.

CHRISTMAS PUDDING

"We gather as an extended family on Christmas Eve and give everyone a dish of pudding. One of the servings has a raisin in it. Whoever gets the raisin gets to open his or her present first."

—Nellee Woodland

BIRTHDAY CAKE, SANTA'S TREAT

Celebrate Christmas as the "birthday" of Jesus Christ. Make a traditional birthday cake to remind the family that Christmas is the day we celebrate His coming into the world. Then, instead of leaving cookies for Santa, leave a slice of Jesus' birthday cake for a treat.

SPECIAL STORIES OR MOVIES

"Our family always watches the video of *Stubby Pringle's Christmas* on Christmas Eve. It is a wonderful story about a cowboy who finds the true meaning of Christmas as he serves a family and helps them to have a Merry Christmas. It just wouldn't be Christmas without it!"

—Jeffrey M. Loveridge

"CHRISTMAS I REMEMBER BEST"

"Every Christmas Eve, our family reads some of our favorite Christmas stories from the 'Christmas I Remember Best' collection from the *Deseret News*. These stories have been in our family for years now, but they always bring tears to our eyes and never get old to us. They always help us to focus on the true meaning of Christmas."

—Jennifer L. Dustin

CHRISTMAS EVE CANDLING

"On Christmas Eve, we 'candled' our children to bed. We would march the kids in a row, each holding a lit candle, and sing carols as we walked to their rooms. We would start with the youngest and go one by one to the bedrooms and 'candle' each child with his or her own carol. We would then blow out that child's candle. After that, they couldn't get up out of bed until morning."

—Kathy Schlendorf

LOAVES AND FISHES

"Every Christmas Eve, we have a traditional meal of 'loaves and fishes' by candlelight in the living room. My mom bakes several boxes of fish sticks, and we spread a big blanket on the floor to sit on. We pass several unsliced loaves of bread around the room, and people tear off pieces for themselves. Then we pass the fish sticks and have our simple meal with water to drink. Afterwards, Dad reads to us from the New Testament about the miracle of the loaves and fishes. We celebrate not just the birth but the life of Jesus, and we have a meaningful discussion about Him."

—Timothy A. Johnson

SPECIAL CHRISTMAS CHINA

"On Christmas Eve we have a family dinner with extended family, taking turns at various homes. We eat on special Christmas plates that have been given as gifts from an aunt over the years. Now we are giving Christmas plates to our own children who have married so that they can carry on this tradition."

—Ann Whittaker

SAVE CHRISTMAS DAY FOR CHRIST

Some families prefer to open gifts on Christmas Eve to preserve Christmas Day for activities of a more sacred nature.

TELEPHONE CAROLING

"Every Christmas Eve, my family, friends, and neighbors go caroling and have a party after we are done. One year, it was too cold in the foothills of Tennessee to go caroling, so we actually called people on the phone and sang to them! The tradition had to be upheld!"

—Lynnae Boyer Weller

CAROLING, CAROLING, NOW WE GO

"On Christmas Eve we go Christmas caroling around the neighborhood. We give jam or banana bread to all the 'old timers,' but anyone new on the street gets a copy of the Book of Mormon."

—Elizabeth Larsen

IMPROMPTU CONCERT

"In our family, my mother and I play 'Sleigh Ride' as a duet on the piano. We are not allowed to practice this difficult piece at any time during the year, and so the family has a good laugh (and so do we) as we 'clink' our way through the piece each year."

—Sally Brinton

TESTIMONY SHARING

Christmas Eve is a great time to have a family testimony meeting. The family will look forward to the spiritual feast with the ones they love the most.

Fun with Santa Claus

Santa plays a very important role in our Christmas celebrating. This jolly old elf adds joy and happiness to the season as the entire family anticipates his visit. We feel that he truly exemplifies the spirit of Christmas giving.

Footboard Stockings

To allow the parents a few extra minutes to sleep in on Christmas morning, have Santa fill the stockings and put them at the foot of each child's bed. Upon awakening, the children will delight in the goodies in their stockings and will have something to enjoy while waiting for Mom and Dad to come and get them to open presents.

Santa's Footprints

Santa isn't always careful in his rush from house to house. Sometimes he can leave big, dirty footprints on the carpet, from the fireplace to the tree. Children love that sort of thing, but moms always seem to be a little upset with him!

Magic Stockings

Santa's magic can exist all during Christmas Day. Have the children place their stockings in a part of the home of their choosing. Somehow, throughout all of Christmas Day, Santa manages to return again and again, unseen, to leave little extra presents in each child's stocking.

Snuggling Pal from Santa

Have Santa make a special visit to each person's bedroom. They will be surprised when they wake up, sometimes in the middle of the night, to discover the stuffed animal they have been snuggling with, a gift generously left by none other than Santa Claus himself.

The Final Touches on the Tree

Decorate the family tree, leaving some bare branches. On Christmas morning, as part of his other "magic," Santa also takes time to finish decorating the family tree, with candy canes and other goodies to eat.

A Gingerbread Snack

In lieu of cookies for Santa, make a huge family gingerbread house, covered in all the most delicious candies. Leave a note for Santa, inviting him to nibble at the gingerbread as he chooses. On Christmas morning, arm the children with hammers to break off the leftovers that Santa didn't take with him.

Santa Writes Back

"We would always leave a note and cookies for Santa and a carrot for Rudolph on the hearth. Santa would always write back!"

—Melanie Bingham

Two-Part Visit from Santa

Have Santa pay a personal visit to the family. As the children take a look outside to see if they can spot Santa and his sleigh, have Santa drop in, leaving one gift and a note that he will return later. When the children return from outside, they will be sorry they missed his initial visit, but will anxiously await Santa's later arrival. Not long after that, have Santa arrive, complete with gifts for each one of the children.

Christmas Day

Our family has found that the true joy of Christmas is in giving. As the Savior has given us the greatest gift of all, we experience that joy of giving through the exchange of love and kindness on Christmas Day. As one of the most anticipated holidays, this special time brings our family closer to each other, and closer to our Savior, with every passing year.

$\mathscr{A}$ Message from the Church

Before opening presents, take a few minutes as a family and read together a talk from one of the General Authorities of the Church. Read a pamphlet specifically about Christmas, or read the First Presidency's Christmas message in the December *Ensign*.

$\mathscr{B}$reakfast Stockings

On Christmas morning, when children are full of anxiety and often don't want to take time to eat breakfast before opening presents, try putting a mini-breakfast in their stockings. Include some fruit, a juice box, and a granola bar as nutritious stocking stuffers.

$\mathscr{J}$ust Like Jesus

To turn the focus away from the commercialism that sometimes accompanies Christmas, create the tradition that every family member receives just three presents, to represent the three presents that Jesus Christ received from the Wise Men.

$\mathscr{H}$andmade Christmas

As Christmas can sometimes be a financial burden to families, adopt the tradition that all family members give only handmade gifts to one another. They will receive greater joy as they open these "gifts of the heart," and the giver will certainly gain a deeper appreciation for the "gift of giving."

CHRISTMAS TREASURE HUNT

Instead of wrapping all of the presents to be placed under the tree, take the family on a treasure hunt. Lead them around the house, and maybe even the neighborhood, with clues until finally they arrive at the place where their treasure lies.

THE BABY'S ARRIVAL

Accent your Christmas decorating with a traditional nativity, minus the baby Jesus. Then, on Christmas morning, add the baby Jesus to the scene, to mirror His arrival on Christmas Day.

HIDDEN ORNAMENT

In the spirit of a German tradition, hide one special ornament on the Christmas tree on Christmas morning. All of the children gather to see who can most quickly spot this particular, and often unusual, ornament. The first child to see it is awarded a prize for being most observant.

VIDEO OF CHRISTMAS PAST

"Gather all your old home movies and snapshots taken at Christmas through the years and transfer them to videotapes. This makes it possible to watch Christmas past as many times as you or your children want and thus be able to remember their favorite Christmases."

—Judy Gill

CHRISTMAS AT THE CABIN

"Ever since our first children were tiny, we have spent the week of Christmas at our cabin near Yellowstone. To prepare for this occasion I shop early and take all the gifts to the cabin over Thanksgiving so that the weeks between Thanksgiving and Christmas are fun and not burdened with hectic shopping. Our family would not want to spend that day anywhere else. Santa always pays a visit to the cabin, and we enjoy all kinds of winter snow activities during the week. One year I forgot to take the gifts, and it really didn't matter, because we discovered that being together as a family was more important than gifts."

—Nancy Hobbs

BREAKFAST BINGE

"Every Christmas morning we have a huge breakfast. We invite our grandparents and siblings, local missionaries, and other neighbors or friends who might be alone on Christmas. My husband, Steve, is the master chef. He cooks the most yummy, made-to-order omelettes for everyone for a full two hours! We visit and have so much fun. Our house is bustling every Christmas morning with holiday cheer! It is the highlight of the season for me."

—Kathie Terry

All On a Christmas Morning

"Each year, we have a tradition of not putting our presents out under the tree until Christmas Day. It creates a much more 'magical' feeling on Christmas morning, and, in the lean years, it helped the children to feel like even a few presents helped to transform the home on Christmas Day."

—Colleen Petersen

First Things First

"Every Christmas morning, before we open presents, we visit an elderly man who doesn't have much family around with whom to celebrate Christmas. We began doing this as small children, and now that we are almost all grown, we still enjoy the yearly visit to his home on Christmas morning."

—Amy L. Hendrickson

Ornament Collection

"We have started the tradition of buying one Christmas tree ornament for each of our children each year and marking them with their names and the years. Not only will the children be able to take several ornaments with them when they marry but they have a lot fun memories, too."

—Janet Davidson

Never-Ending Meal

"We spend Christmas Day with my husband's family. The day-long affair begins at noon, and we travel to visit each one of his relatives, eating a full meal at each home and staying there to visit for an hour or two. By 10:00 P.M. the traveling party is over, and we have eaten dinner a half-dozen times. We are stuffed, but happy."

—Kathy Cahoon

Two Are Better Than One

"Because I come from such a large family, we have two Christmas parties every year. The first one is for everyone, and this is on Christmas Day. The other party is for adults only, and is held two days after Christmas."

—Jan Marshall

Scripture Study

Establishing this important practice leads to great habits for all family members. We have learned that the scriptures bring us closer together and help us get through the trials that we face in this life. Some of the greatest spiritual experiences we have shared as a family have happened during this special study time.

Read for Your Supper

"Once a month, assign a section of scriptures to the family to be read by the end of the month. On the last day, take the family out to dinner. Each member of the family must account for the chapters that he or she read the previous month. If they have read the entire section of scripture, they will be allowed to order an entire meal. If they have read only parts of the required reading, then they will be allowed to order only one or more of the following: beverage, salad, soup, appetizer, or dinner, depending on what they finished reading. (Dessert should be saved for those who have read everything!)"

—Debi Wilcox

Scripture Block

Decide on a weekly scripture block, and have family members read that block individually on their own time. Meet once a week to discuss the block of scripture that the entire family has read, and talk about the insights that the family members got from their own personal study.

Listen Together

When there are small children as well as teenagers in the home, the audiotapes of the Book of Mormon are sometimes helpful. The older children can follow along in their own personal sets of scriptures, and the smaller children can listen closely for words and phrases that they recognize.

Two Thumbs Up

"When our children were very small, we thought of some new ways to hold their interest during scripture time. Whenever we would read the phrase 'And it came to ___,' we would pause for the kids to say 'pass.' We also play 'thumbs up,' where the children put their thumbs up if they hear anything good in the scriptures like 'Heavenly Father,' 'Christ,' or 'Holy Ghost.' They put their thumbs down if they hear any wickedness. This has definitely been a big tradition in our home. Even when the cousins come for a sleepover, they know just what to do."

—Barry and Lucie Gibbons

Traveling Scriptures

When families are especially busy and have many time constraints away from each other, they may benefit from listening to Book of Mormon tapes in the car. This will certainly help to keep the stress level down while giving a great spiritual boost to the day.

For the Family

Purchase a copy of *The Book of Mormon for Latter-day Saint Families* to enhance scripture study for smaller children and teenagers alike. This unique book helps explain difficult passages and accents scriptures with applicable quotes and insights from prophets and scholars.

SCRIPTURES AROUND THE HOUSE

Try putting scriptures in prominent places in the home where the children will see them every day. This is especially helpful when the family doesn't have much time together in the mornings or evenings for joint study. Tape blocks of scripture on cereal boxes or on bathroom mirrors. Plastic page protectors can even allow you to put them in the shower.

ILLUSTRATED SCRIPTURE STORIES

Break up a specific story or parable in the scriptures, and have each member of the family illustrate one piece of the story. Later, tape the drawings together in chronological order, and scroll through the pictures while retelling the story or parable. Children will certainly remember the stories better after having participated in illustrating them.

BREAKFAST READING

"In a house where children all seem to be going different ways at any time of the day, I found that breakfast was an especially great time for our family to get in our scripture study. Sometimes I would just read to the kids as they ate, if they didn't have the time to follow along. It was a good way for them to start their day before I sent them out the door into the world."

—Susan Monson

TOPICAL SCRIPTURE STUDY

Study by topic. Go through the Topical Guide or index in the scriptures and choose a subject. Have different members of the family look up one reference at a time until all of the references to a specific subject have been studied. Follow up with testimonies of family members explaining why that principle is important to them.

SCRIPTURES IN ACTION

"Once a month, after we had family scripture study, we would get together and act out a parable or story from the scriptures while my parents videotaped. We had a great time learning how to bring the scriptures to life, and we truly learned and remembered those stories because we had participated in them."

—Jennifer L. Dustin

SCRIPTURAL JOURNEY

"Our family likes to have scripture treasure hunts. We all are led on a hunt with scriptures for clues to help us get to the next spot. We learn how to interpret the scriptures, and so we get a great spiritual treasure to add to the one at the end of the trail."

—Trent Thomas

SCRIPTURAL DIGESTION

"Every morning before my kids leave for school, I have them go over an Article of Faith or scripture. It takes only about three to five minutes and has proved to be very beneficial in helping them to memorize. We also study the twelve apostles' names matched with their faces."

—Catherine Ellis

Mealtime

We have learned that the most important thing about mealtime is that we actually have it together! This time provides a great opportunity for us to bond as we hear about each other's day and give counsel and advice to one another concerning any problems.

A Time To Learn

Use mealtime as a place to teach manners and table etiquette. Set a formal table at every meal, and teach the family what each fork and spoon is used for. Practice folding napkins in special ways, and occasionally cook different foods that require special instructions for eating.

Personal Plates

Make individualized plates for each member of the family. Decorate them according to the talents and preferences of the family members. At special family meals, use these plates to help each person to feel the importance of his or her place in the family.

A Trip Down Memory Lane

Each time the family gathers together for a meal, go around the table and have each person begin a sentence with, "I remember when . . ." It will be fun for the entire family to reminisce about the times they shared growing up, and may provide a few laughs before the meal is served.

Cooking Kids

Have each person in the family take a turn during the week to make dinner for the rest of the family. Include menu planning, shopping for ingredients, setting the table, and cooking the food. The children will all gain a better appreciation for Mom's efforts; they'll also learn some useful tricks for when they are on their own.

DINNER BELL

Use a bell or other signal to warn family members when dinner is about five or ten minutes from being ready. Then, when dinner is served, sound the bell again. All family members should be seated within two minutes of the final bell or must wait to eat until the rest of the family is finished. (Mom will never again have to serve a meal that has gotten cold from waiting for everyone to sit down!)

DINING SPOTS

Take an evening for family members to make their own individual place mats. Have them decorate them in any way that they want. At mealtime, let the person setting the table choose where each person will sit, as designated by the arrangement of the place mats. This allows everyone to get a chance to sit by someone new each meal.

WEEKLONG MENU

"In our home, Mom always had a set menu for breakfast. I think it made things easier on her, but it also gave the children something to look forward to on specific days. We had hot cereal on Monday, Wednesday, and Friday, but enjoyed French toast, omelettes, or pancakes on Tuesday and Thursday."

—Jeffrey M. Loveridge

Manners Paid Off

Have different ways of choosing who gets to help with dessert. It may be the person who first remembers to put a napkin on his or her lap, or the one who first compliments the chef on the dinner. This helps the entire family be on their best behavior every night to see who will be allowed the privilege of being dubbed "dessert disher."

Dinner Potpourri

"Once a month, we have what we call the 'take-what-comes dinner.' Each person in the family is assigned to bring something to the table that sounds appealing to him or her. We then sit down and just eat 'what comes.'"

—Becky Crockett

Lunchtime, Quiet Time

"Our family established a habit of having lunch together and then sharing some quiet time. During that time, I read to my children. I put a sign on the door to let the neighbor children know that we will be out soon."

—Jim and Diane Toronto

Table of Wisdom

"In our family, we have a clear plastic tablecloth over our regular tablecloth. Underneath the plastic, I can place quotes or special notes that the children will be sure to see. Because of the plastic, there is no worry over spills messing up the messages."

—Sherry Simmerman

Baptism

The occasion of baptism is a significant time, and our family has always treated it with extra attention. The focus on the individual makes it an event to be remembered for a lifetime by the entire family. We involve extended family members as often as possible to keep those ties close.

DRESSED FOR THE OCCASION

When children are baptized and become members of the Church, take them out and buy them a new outfit for the Sabbath day. Impress upon your children the importance of keeping the Sabbath day holy, and explain that their outward appearance reflects their testimony of the Lord's holy day.

FIRST FAST

In anticipation of becoming a new member of the Church, have your child fast, and teach the importance of coming closer to the Spirit through fasting and prayer. Share your testimony with your child, and invite him or her to do the same, after the fasting is concluded.

BAPTISMAL GIFT

For baptism, give a special gift to your children that they will receive only upon their baptism. It may be a piece of jewelry, a picture of the Savior to hang in their bedroom, or a special picture of themselves in front of the temple.

CHOOSE A RESTAURANT

Allow the child who is being baptized to choose a restaurant where the family can go to celebrate his or her new membership in the Church. This outing may include the entire family, or it may be a special date for the child to go out alone with Mom and Dad.

$\mathcal{A}$ Family Legacy

When a child is baptized, invite the other previously baptized members of the family, both immediate and extended, to write their testimonies down, and include them in a special binder to be presented to the child the night before the baptism.

$\mathcal{W}$ritten Record

A journal is a great gift to give a child at baptism. The baptism day would make a great first entry, as the new Church member writes his or her fresh and maturing testimony.

$\mathcal{F}$rame the Day

Give your child a special frame that has some significance to the baptism. It may be a homemade one with "CTR" painted on the border, or one from a store with a special meaning to the child. Be sure to put the pictures from the baptism day in that frame for the child to look at often as a reminder of the covenants made at baptism.

$\mathcal{H}$eirloom Dress

"In our family, we have a very special baptism dress that has been handed down through the generations. All of the daughters and granddaughters have been baptized in the same dress."

—Elizabeth Larsen

ℒETTERS FROM GRANDPARENTS

"We try to make our children's baptisms very special occasions that they will always remember. We ask the grandparents to write special letters to the children, and we give the children their own sets of scriptures with their names printed on them."

—Lou Ellen Romrell

ℬECOMING CONVERTED

Before a child is baptized, invite the local missionaries to teach the discussions in your home. Explain to the child the importance of gaining a personal testimony of the gospel as a step toward baptism. Have the missionaries invite the child to read the Book of Mormon, as they would any person they would teach, and follow through with the lessons until they are completed.

Twelfth Birthday

Twelve years of age is a turning point, particularly in Latter-day Saint culture, for both young men and young women. As they advance into new programs, and as boys receive the priesthood, we have tried in our family to stress the importance of their increasing responsibility with age and the significance of this time in their lives.

Dressed to Fit

When children turn twelve and enter into the youth program of the Church, give them a new set of Church clothing to distinguish them from the Primary-aged children. This may include a new suit and tie for the young men, and a new dress for the young women.

Priesthood Blessing

At the time of this special birthday, give your children the gift of a priesthood blessing. As they move from Primary into the Young Men's or Young Women's program, reassure them of their place in the Lord's plan, and of their increasing responsibility as one of the "youth of the noble birthright."

Beehive Cake

When young women enter into the Young Women's program at the age of twelve, bake them a special "beehive" cake (a cake baked in a heart-shaped pan and then displayed upside down works well) to encourage them to be industrious, like the bee, and to support the program as a member of that organization.

Embossed Scriptures

When young men and young women turn twelve years of age, get them a new set of scriptures with the word "Elder" or "Sister" imprinted in front of their names, as a reminder of their commitment to the gospel and to the title that they should carry throughout their lives.

Joining the Flock

"When a boy turns twelve, my father always flies with him to Utah (we're from Illinois) to see the priesthood session of general conference in person. It was great to spend time with Dad and learn the importance of the Aaronic Priesthood."

—Alvin Van Orden

Boys' Night Out

After the priesthood session, have all of the priesthood holders in the family join together for a night out. Enjoy dinner before conference or dessert afterwards. Take the time to impress upon the younger boys the importance of being part of the great force of priesthood holders in the Lord's church.

First Temple Trip

"For each of our children, with the help of good bishops, we have surprised our twelve-year-olds by taking them to the temple to do baptisms on their twelfth birthdays. We arise very early and take all family members who are twelve and older. It's been a sweet thing to watch them have a love for temple work at such a young age."

—Barry and Lucie Gibbons

Mission and Temple Endowment

As family members reach the milestones of receiving their own temple endowments and going on missions, we share in the joy and excitement of watching them take the next step in their eternal progression. We find these occasions to be great teaching moments for younger children. When we can point out the examples of those older family members, it brings home the importance of the temple and eternal families.

Temple Symbolism

After people have received their endowments, they may be interested in knowing some of the history behind many of the things that they learned in the temple. Give them a book explaining some of the symbols of the ancient temples.

Showered with Love

After a missionary has accepted his or her call to serve, have a "missionary shower" with the extended family. "Shower" the missionary with things he or she will need as a servant of the Lord: shirts, ties, socks, skirts, sweaters, journals, stamps, stationery, and so on.

Vision of Things to Come

When a child decides to serve a mission, invite the missionaries into the home to teach the discussions to the family. It will give the prospective missionary a better understanding of what he or she will be doing over the next couple of years, as well as strengthen testimony.

A New Frontier

When a missionary has learned where he or she will be serving, have a special family home evening in which each member of the family prepares to share a few facts about the country or state where the prospective missionary will be going.

TEMPLE TOUR

"The week before I went on my mission, my dad went with me out to Utah on a temple tour. We saw one or two temples every day. It was a great chance to gain a testimony of the temple and get spiritual advice from my dad before leaving for two years. My mom did the same thing when my sisters went out on their missions."

—Alvin Van Orden

MISSIONARY BULLETIN BOARD

"As a grandmother, I like to honor those members of my family who have dedicated their time to the Lord as full-time missionaries. I display their pictures, along with mission information, in a large picture frame, which hangs in my kitchen for all my visitors to see. The grandchildren see this board and feel inspired to be a part of it by serving a mission."

—Beth Mikkelson

MISSIONARY FAMILY HOME EVENING

"We write a joint letter to a missionary recounting our favorite family nights we've ever had. Everyone picks a memory and tells about the lesson, games we played, and songs we sang. It is always interesting because everyone's is different. Now the missionary has six family night lessons that he can present to a family he is teaching."

—Kristine Dallimore Bytheway

Traveling Tie

"Our first son kept one of his faithful missionary ties. His brother took the 'family tie' with him on his mission, too. The next brother is looking forward to his turn with the tie, and maybe someday Dad will use the tie when he and Mom serve a mission."

—Randi Nuila

Serve According to the Call

As your missionaries receive their calls to serve, take them out to dinner at a restaurant that features cuisine to match that of the country where they will be serving.

Mission Bricks

"While the boys of our family were on their missions we had bricks laser-inscribed stating their names, missions, and dates they left and returned. When they came back we gave them the bricks and they chose their own spots to insert them into our brick patio. We also have a brick stating when residence was established, and look forward to adding marriage and grandchild bricks."

—Randi Nuila

Sunday Activities

We look forward to the Sabbath as a day of bonding and sharing. In the absence of television, computer, and other outside worldly influences, we have found the peaceful spirit that dwells in our home allows us to create loving and spiritual memories together, more than on any other day of the week.

Journal Writing

Sunday afternoons are a great time to sit down at the table as a family and write in journals. When the children are young, have them dictate to Mom or Dad, who then write down all of the thoughts and feelings of young minds.

Father's Interview

Once a month, have a personal father's interview with each member of the family (including Mom). This will be a great opportunity to keep track of each person's spiritual, emotional, and even social progress.

Church Meeting Thank-You

After church, sit down as a family and discuss the things that you learned in sacrament meeting. Together, compose thank-you cards for the people who spoke, mentioning specific things that you appreciated about their messages. You might even take a small treat along with your notes to the people who made a difference in your Sabbath meetings.

Family Home Evening Planner

Use Sunday afternoon as a time to plan the following Monday night's family home evening. Assign different family members to give prayers, talks, songs, and special numbers. As a family, decide what the topic could be for the evening.

Sunday Night Family Night

Once a month, get together with extended family members for a joint family home evening. Teach a lesson appropriate for all ages, and take the time to celebrate birthdays in the family for that month. This will keep the children close to their grandparents, aunts, uncles, and cousins.

General Family Conference

After general conference concludes, take that Sunday evening to recap the talks that were given. Assign family members to give highlights of different talks throughout the conference from notes they have taken during the sessions. Try to include at least one thought from each talk given.

Sounds of Sunday

On the Sabbath day, have appropriate music playing in your home to invite the Spirit and help it remain throughout the day. This will be a great reminder and help to the family to "keep the Sabbath day holy."

Sunday Surprise

On Sunday morning, give your children a little something to look forward to, to help them feel like Sunday really is a special day, apart from the others during the week. Place a small mint or candy underneath their pillows for them to have a sweet awakening.

DAD COOKS

On Sunday morning, when Mom seems to have so much to do to get all the children dressed and ready, Dad can make breakfast for the family. It will be fun for the children to sample Dad's cuisine for a change, and will give Mom a morning of rest.

ACCEPTABLE ACTIVITY LIST

Have a list posted in the family room or other common area with some acceptable ideas for Sunday activities. Children will then have a clear idea of some things that they can do, instead of wandering around wondering what there is to do.

SATURDAY IS A SPECIAL DAY

"Growing up with four other sisters, Sunday morning tended to be a bit stressful to our mother, who tried to get us all ready and do our hair. She always laid our clothing out on our dressers on Saturday night, so at least on Sunday morning we were never looking for lost shoes or trying to find a clean dress to wear."

—Amy L. Hendrickson

SUNDAE SUNDAY

"Each month on a certain Sunday, our family looks forward to having ice-cream sundaes. It has become a great tradition that we call 'Sundae Sunday.'"

—Kaye Swallow

Sunday Activity Box

"In our home, we have a box that we pull out only on Sundays. It is full of activities that are appropriate for the Sabbath Day. Each week, while we are at home, whenever the children need something to do that will help us to keep the day holy, we pull out our activity box."

—Robin Gunnell

Missionary Sunday

"It has been a tradition at our home to have returned missionaries in our extended family, and also in the ward, come to our home for a family home evening and share their missionary experiences with our family."

—Ruth Egan

Sunday Night Treat

"My husband's family has the tradition of gathering at his mother's house every Sunday evening and eating toast, jam, and cheese. We eat this treat every Sunday at Grandma's house, and if she is not at home, then we eat it at our own house."

—Jeanne English

At Work in the Home

A successful household is one where everyone contributes. Even very young children like the sense of accomplishment that comes from cleaning, helping, and being responsible. When we are working together as a family, the work becomes less of a chore and more of a chance for us to talk and bond together.

Room Check

Assign each child in the home an area that he or she is "in charge" of keeping clean. Whenever a bathroom needs a shine or a floor needs a scrub, the assigned people must mind their stewardships to keep those areas clean. At night, before you go to bed, announce "Room Check" and give the family members ten minutes to tidy up their areas before you inspect them. When the work is finally satisfactory, the family can join for prayer and scriptures and then retire in a clean house.

Litter Laundry Basket

Whenever a family member leaves personal belong-ings around the home, collect them into the Litter Laundry Basket. The person must then "earn back" those items, either by working for them or by buying them back. This should provide enough incentive for the family members to take care of their things and put them back in their places.

Job Box

Create a box with two compartments for each child in the family. One compartment will hold cards of jobs to be done, and the other compartment will hold cards of jobs completed. In the morning, Mom sorts through the cards and gives each child a few cards showing different jobs to be finished around the house. The children must do their "card chores" before anything else that day.

Checking It Twice

Make up checklists, one for each room in your home. Write down every single job you can think of that could ever possibly be done in that room. Keep a dozen copies of each list. Then, on chore day, check off on one copy of the list only those jobs that need to be done that week in that particular room. (Some jobs, such as waxing the floor, need to be done only occasionally.) The children must then complete all the jobs that were checked on the list before they are rewarded.

All in a Day's Work

When there are many people living under one roof, laundry can seem like a huge undertaking. When children are old enough, teach them how to do their own laundry; then assign each person his or her own day to do laundry. Have them collect their own laundry in their own hampers in their bedrooms. They are allowed to use the washer and dryer only on their specific day to minimize the laundry-room traffic jams.

Two by Two

Pair family members up to get the job done. Whenever there is someone there working by your side, the work always seems to go faster, and it is definitely more fun. You may have to keep an extra close eye on them, however, because too much fun may lead to no work done.

Busy as Bees

"In our home, Mom always posted a 'busy bee' on our door while we were doing our chores. This way, we were never interrupted by neighborhood children wanting to play before our work was completed. This bee carried a poem that we all helped Mom to write:

"The Loveridge children are busy as bees
They're helping their mother clean.
They're washing the dishes and folding the clothes
And running the washing machine.
So please don't disturb them by ringing the bell.
They're reading and sweeping the floor.
You're welcome to call on them some other time
When the busy bee's not on the door.

"I remember one time, in fact, when we forgot to place the bee on the door, and one of the neighbor children came calling. Mom simply told him that we were working, and he responded with a bit of indignation, 'Well, why isn't the bee on the door?'"

—Carrie N. Loveridge

By Example

Take time to teach children how each job in the home should be done. Sit beside them and show them step-by-step how to complete the job correctly. Then, the next time, allow the children to do the job by themselves, but check afterward to make sure it was done right.

Line upon Line

Try working as a family at perfecting one area in the home at a time. Decide on an area that needs improvement, such as keeping the microwave wiped out and clean, and work as a family at having a perfect track record in that area. When the family has mastered one area, choose another one, and slowly perfect the home, one section at a time.

We Love the Dishes

Assign each family member a day to be in charge of doing the dishes. It can be an individual effort, or they can have the day paired up with Mom or Dad. At any rate, it will cut the dish time in half for Mom and Dad and will help foster a greater appreciation for those who usually do the dishes for everyone else. Have some fun music playing that they can sing along with to make the work go faster.

Without a Trace

"I remember learning that when we used a room in the home, particularly the bathroom, we should leave it as clean as we found it. That meant wiping off any stray droplets of water on the faucets, and straightening the towels when we were done. It was almost a game to see if we could leave the room perfect, as if we had never been in there."

—Jennifer L. Dustin

Assorted Chores

"Every Saturday, we do our chores in a different way. Here are a few variations:

"a. Charlie Brown—In *A Charlie Brown Christmas,* the kids all turn around and decorate the tree really fast, all together. We do that with whatever room needs straightening, and then we go to the next room, all working together.

"b. I write down the chores on a piece of paper and cut each one out. I fold them and put them in a hat. The kids choose two or three slips of paper, and those are their chores for the day. They usually trade and barter, though!

"c. I put the chores I want them to do in a word search. They find their chores to be done!

"d. I give them a penny for each thing they pick up. My younger children still buy into this one, but the older children want more money!"

—Kristine Dallimore Bytheway

A Cleaning Exercise

"We used to go jogging as a family for our health, but we added a little twist. I had each person in the family carry a garbage bag, and as we saw trash along the way, we would pick it up and put it in our bags. We kept our bodies healthy and helped in our neighborhood as well."

—Nellee Woodland

Den Chief Helper

As in the Scouting program, choose one chief helper to "oversee" and manage the work of the others. Take turns being in charge.

Your Chores Are Numbered

"In our family, we write down a list of chores, and then number them. We put the numbers in a hat and have the children draw out their chores for the day. It makes a game out of what would otherwise be just plain 'work.'"

—Keith and Teresa Ramsey

Vacations

A family vacation provides a wonderful opportunity for anticipation and planning as a family. The trips we have taken have become unique times to be together without the daily stresses of school and work and chores, where we can laugh, joke, and play, twenty-four hours a day.

Travel Games

There are many fun car games that will help to keep the family in good spirits as you are traveling. Try playing the "alphabet game": Look on billboards and license plates for letters of the alphabet, in order from A to Z. The first person to get through the entire alphabet wins. This also works for numbers.

License Plate Phrases

While traveling, try to make sentences or phrases in which each word begins with one of the letters on the license plates around you. For example, the license-plate letters "G J Y" could be "Green Jell-O's Yummy." Try to be the first person to blurt out the three-word phrase, and you will come up with some very funny and sometimes absurd sentences. It will keep the family entertained for a long time.

Who Needs Technology?

"As we traveled with our two daughters on many vacations through the years, we learned that we could have a wonderful bonding experience because we didn't allow video games or television in the car. Consequently, we actually talked and laughed and shared many feelings while traveling. The sights we saw were interesting, but the highlight was the good feelings we had about each other as we talked and shared."

—Laura Green

TRAVEL TREAT BOX

"I purchased small divided plastic containers for each child and labeled them with names and pictures. The day or so before each trip, I take the children to the grocery store and let them each choose two small food treats. At home, we divide the treats up and share with each other, putting them in the divided compartments. Each plastic container goes on a child's seat, and the children get to eat from one compartment at a specific point along the way."

—CheRee Tanner

"MY BLANKEE"

If there is room, allow each child to have his or her own blanket in the car to snuggle with and wrap up in when they are sleepy. It gives them a soft place to rest their heads until you stop the car.

MISSION MEMORIES

A family naturally bonds through a relative's mission experiences. Take a vacation to visit a family member's mission area. Perhaps you could visit Dad's old mission, or brother's last area. Bring along the mission letters to read as you visit different places of significance for the missionary. Take time to share testimonies as a family on the importance of missionary work, both as full-time missionaries and as families of missionaries.

A Day Outdoors

"When we were children, we used to spend the day in the canyon. Mom would pack food, and at dawn, we would all drive up the canyon and cook a 'sunrise' breakfast. We spent the day hiking, napping, discovering, and playing. We roasted hot dogs and ate fresh fruit for lunch, then played and explored some more. For supper, we made our own tin-foil dinners, roasted marshmallows, and sang songs accompanied by Mom's guitar. Those little day trips to the canyon were some of my very favorite experiences as a child."

—Jeffrey M. Loveridge

Olympic Parks

As the Summer and Winter Olympic Games are of worldwide interest, take vacations to visit different Olympic parks, to celebrate the accomplishments and achievements of athletes and medalists of the world. Ride the luge, swim in the Olympic pools, and skate on the ice rinks. Collect pins and memorabilia to show your support for these special events.

Behavior Bucks

"Whenever we travel, we play cooperation games. If the children behave and play well together, we reward them with dollars to buy goodies for the road."

—Cheryl Linford

Books on Tape

As an alternative to television and videos during travel, get a book on tape to entertain the entire family. Listening to a book can be an enriching, educational experience while passing the time on those long stretches of freeway. You will be amazed at how interested the children are in the stories, and at what a great exercise it is for their minds to use their imaginations.

A Time to Share

A time-share vacation home could be a more afford-able alternative to owning vacation property. Some time-share programs allow you to visit different parts of the world at different times of the year. Hotels can be expensive, and eating out at restaurants can become costly, but with a time-share you enjoy the convenience of "home-style" living while on vacation.

Museum Day

Take a museum vacation. Visit different museums to appeal to the different ages and interests of the family members. Visit a pioneer museum, natural history museum, children's museum, art museum, church history museum, or antique museum. Talk together as a family about the importance of preserving the present for future generations as you show appreciation for those who did this in the past.

How Many Questions?

Play twenty questions by thinking of something and allowing everyone to ask yes-or-no questions about it to see if they can guess what you are thinking of. If they can't guess in twenty questions, the person who thought of the thing wins! This is a great game to keep drivers awake on long, late trips.

Fun for Rent

Sometimes the cost of recreational vehicles can seem out of reach, but the cost to rent is really quite affordable for the occasional play day on vacation. Four-wheelers, Jet Skis, and Wave Runners are fun and require little expertise or practice for an exciting day for the whole family. Many companies offer these "toys" for rent right on-site at different resorts and parks.

Just Around the Corner

Vacations don't need to be elaborate or expensive. Take some time to visit your own city as if you were a tourist. Visit some of the historical and fascinating sites close to home, and "rediscover" the place where you live. Talk about the people who built the city, and study some of the architecture that has stood through the ages. Sample some of the local cuisine. You might even purchase some souvenirs from your adventure.

Splish Splash

Go down to the water. Whether you live near the ocean or near a lake, or simply have a community pool nearby, take the time as a family to swim, splash, and soak. Take along a boat where all can help paddle, or bring a canoe for everyone to practice their balancing! Enjoy lunch at the water's edge, perhaps even eating the "catch of the day" from the lake.

Movie Buffs

If your family enjoys movies, take a summer day to attend the cinema all day long! You may want to begin with a mini lesson discussing the movie standards outlined by the Church in the *For the Strength of Youth* pamphlet. Then allow each member of the family to choose a movie that he or she would like to see, so that every member's tastes are represented. Make sure to include lunch and snack times so as to keep up your strength between features! This plan also works with videos in the comfort of your own family room at home.

Hot-Air Balloon

For something a little out of the ordinary, take a hot-air balloon ride. Every member of the family will enjoy the excitement of peacefully floating through the sky in the cool, calm air, high above the world below. Don't forget the camera for this incredible experience!

CHURCH HISTORY TOUR

Plan as a family to travel to Church history sites and track the progress of the growth of the Church. Start in Vermont and visit the place where Joseph Smith was born; then go to the homes where he grew up, had the First Vision, and translated the Book of Mormon. Follow the trail of the pioneers as they came west to Utah. Not only will you gain an appreciation for the sacrifices of the first members of the Church but you will increase in family testimony and spirituality.

PARK-A-THON

"My husband figured that there are roughly four hundred national parks, national monuments, and historical monuments throughout the United States. We decided that as a family we would like to visit every single one. Every vacation that we take, we map out all the national sites on our vacation route, and then check them off as we visit each one. We feel that the children are learning all about the beauty of God's creations and about the importance of preserving the earth."

—ElLois Wilson Bailey

SING YOUR WAY HOME

Gather the words to camp songs and other favorites, and make small books to keep in the car. The children will love to sing together during long trips, and they can begin to learn singing in parts.

A Summer of Saturdays

"Many Saturdays in the summer, when Dad didn't have to work, we would pack a lunch and pile into the car with no idea of where we were going. Then, Dad would just start driving. We would sometimes end up at a nearby park to play tennis or volleyball, but sometimes we would climb high mountains or even cross the border into a neighboring state. As we visited different places, we gained a great appreciation for the beautiful country we have."

—Robert E. Hales

Treasury Trip

Have the family work together to earn money for the family vacation. Allow the children to choose a place that they would like to visit; then let them pitch in some of their allowance and other loose change to help pay for a part of the vacation.

Vacation in a Day

When different members of a family have conflicting schedules, it may be hard to find an entire week in which to take a family vacation. So, just take a day-long vacation! For one day, take the phone off the hook or leave the house altogether. Do an art project together, go to a park, or drive to a nearby canyon. It doesn't matter what you do, as long as you are all together, creating memories.

CRUISIN'

"It had never occurred to me to take a cruise with our family. That seemed like something that retired couples do after all of their children are out of the home. But one of the best vacations I remember was going on a cruise with my family to the Caribbean. I had to work hard to earn enough money to go, but in the end it was well worth the effort. We snorkeled, danced, watched plays, played games, and shopped together. It was a memorable time for all of us."

—Amy L. Hendrickson

ANNUAL CAMPING

"Every year, I plan an extended family camping trip by a lake. I reserve a week at a campsite that we all grew up visiting, and then the various families are invited to spend as much or as little time as they wish during that week. We sleep in tents and take turns cooking meals so that we are all well fed! The cousins have a great time fishing, hiking, star gazing, and swimming; they look forward to our annual campout every year."

—Jeri Benson

RIDER'S ARITHMETIC

For younger kids learning their math facts, have them see who can add up the numbers in a license plate and shout out the answer first. This keeps them entertained while they're sharpening their math skills.

WHAT CHARMING STATES!

"When our daughters were young, we took advantage of our vacation time to travel to as many different states as possible to learn about their own special sites and history. Each daughter had a charm bracelet and was allowed to choose a special charm to purchase from the different states we visited. These state charms have become wonderful memorabilia of our fun times together."

—Laura Green

SHHHHH . . .

Play the "quiet game." Tell the children (and they usually have to be pretty young to fall for this) that you are having a contest to see who can be the most quiet. They will try to keep all of their moves silent, and Mom and Dad will certainly enjoy the peaceful ride.

ON THE STREET WHERE YOU LIVED

"One year on a family vacation, Dad took us to the town in Wisconsin where he grew up. We visited the home and schools he attended. As we drove and walked around, Dad shared many wonderful stories of his childhood in that area. The highlight of the trip was learning more about Dad and feeling closer to him as we visited and saw the places that contributed to making him the person he is today."

—Timothy A. Johnson

On the Road Again

"One of our family's favorite ways to vacation is in a motor home. When we were young children, my parents rented a motor home and took us to California. It was such a positive and fun experience that they continued to rent one almost every year to travel to different destinations. The best part about it was that once we left our driveway, we were already on vacation because the fun began immediately! We played games, cooked food, sang songs, and talked or took a nap. Even now that most of us are married with our own children, Mom and Dad still take us on extended family trips in a motor home."

—Carrie N. Loveridge

Birthdays

Birthdays are an important part of growing up in our family. We try to make birthdays special so that our family members know how much we love them and what a valuable part of our family they are. Everyone in our family looks forward to our birthday celebrations, even when it's someone else's birthday!

DECK THE HALLS

Create a "party box" filled with balloons, streamers, and birthday hats that can be used to decorate for any family member's birthday. Children delight in hanging decorations, and especially in seeing the things hung in their honor.

GRANDPARENT VACATION

Vacations are always special, especially when you travel with those you love. To increase the bond across generations, it might be fun to plan for grandparents to take a grandchild on a vacation alone for a certain "milestone" birthday. This can be exotic or low-key, but the child is certain to remember the relationship long after the memory of the birthday fades.

WAKE UP AND SMELL THE . . .

Surprise the birthday boy or girl with breakfast in bed. Whip up all of the person's favorites and gather the entire family to deliver the meal while singing "Happy Birthday." What a great way to start the day!

THE GROUND YOU WALK ON

Purchase some sidewalk chalk and send your birthday wishes to members of your family on the walkways leading to their car, school, or work. Get creative with colors and pictures. The message can extend for a few feet or for several yards if you wish!

Special Delivery

It is always fun to receive presents, but especially when they arrive at the time you least expect them! Surprise your children by having birthday treats delivered to them at school or work to help them feel extra special on their day.

A Very Merry Unbirthday

Get in the habit of recognizing the family's half-birthdays. This is especially great when a child's birthday falls near to or on a national holiday. This way, those birthday children get a day all to themselves. Try making a half of a cake, and singing every other word to "Happy Birthday."

My Choice!

Allow the birthday child to choose a restaurant or to request his or her favorite dish or menu for dinner. The child can choose where everyone sits at the table and be "in charge" for the evening.

Red Plate

Purchase a red plate to be placed on the dinner table for the birthday child to help him or her feel special and important. This plate can also be used for other important events in a child's life, or to celebrate simple achievements such as saying a prayer, scripture, or talk in Primary, performing in a recital, and so on.

Sweet Sixteen

"In our family, my parents rewarded us on our sixteenth birthday with a hundred-dollar bill if we had never been kissed. It was really something to work toward, and a great joy to accomplish."

—Carrie N. Loveridge

How Do They Measure Up?

Have a tradition of measuring the children's height on their birthdays. Have them stand against a hidden wall or doorframe in the home, and mark each child's height and age with a pen or pencil. They will have fun comparing how they have grown from year to year and seeing how they "measure up" in the family.

Sneaky Elves

When the children are young and sound sleepers, after they have gone to sleep the night before their birthday, go in quietly and decorate their room while they are asleep. Hide treats around the room as an extra surprise for when they awaken.

It's My Day, Too!

"I was born on Christmas, so my parents always had two trees: one for Jesus, and one for me. Christmas gifts went under one tree, and birthday gifts under the other. We continue the tradition today in our home."

—Brad Wilcox

Lift That Bar!

For an extra birthday gift that's greatly anticipated, make up a story about the birthday person and write it on a poster board with candy bars taped into places for missing words (Snickers, Big Hunk, Almond Joy, Baby Ruth, Butterfinger, Chunky, Smarties, Milky Way, Reese's Pieces, 100 Grand, and so on). The birthday child can enjoy this hefty poster for weeks to come.

How Many Is That?

Because smaller children have a harder time appreciating the gifts they are given, try giving them one present for every year of age, up to age six or eight. These can be simple gifts, such as a box of the child's favorite cereal, a packet of punch powder, or a package of Band-Aids. Dollar stores also have a wide variety of gift items to please little ones.

Scrapbooking, Anyone?

"On my boys' birthdays, I create blank birthday pages that I can later slide into their scrapbooks. Then, I invite each member of the extended family to write a short note or fond memory about that child that he can look back on and read when he is older. They might not appreciate it now, but will certainly enjoy looking back on their childhood through the eyes of their loved ones when they are older."

—Tiffany L. Johnson

RIDDLE TREASURE HUNT

"Our family does treasure hunts for hidden birthday gifts. The hunt starts off with one clue and the birthday child gets to try to guess the answer to each successive riddle to find the birthday presents at the end of the hunt. (This actually takes less time than wrapping gifts.)"

—Randi Nuila

WINDOW ART

"A tradition in our family that Mom started when we were very young was to paint our large picture window in the front of our home for our birthdays. It was a way for all the neighborhood to know that we were celebrating our special day. We have even taken up painting the window to surprise Mom on her birthday as well!"

—Amy L. Hendrickson

BIRTHDAY-ONLY CAKE

"In our family, we have a special recipe for a cake that we make only on birthdays. We take two full rectangle cakes and sandwich whipped cream, strawberries, and vanilla ice cream between them. Then, we continue to heap more whipped cream, strawberries, and ice cream on top. This has become something that every family member looks forward to at birthday time."

—Timothy A. Johnson

All to Myself

"On birthdays, our children get to have one whole day alone with Mom (sometimes Dad is invited) and to choose whatever they want to do (skiing, movies, shopping, or whatever)."

—Sharlene Hawkes

Your Reward

"We have a tradition in my family that if a person has totally abstained from drugs, tobacco, and alcohol, he or she receives a gold watch upon turning twenty-one years of age."

—Clayton and Elizabeth Dunford

Facts of Life

"When a child reaches the appropriate age, we plan a special night out with Mom and Dad during which we talk to our children about the facts of life. First, it's off to a favorite restaurant. We then travel to the Bountiful Temple grounds, where we can enjoy a beautiful view of the Lord's house. After a word of prayer to invoke the Spirit, we share the plan of salvation and the importance of families in that plan. The specifics of each of these sweet opportunities have been somewhat different, based on the promptings of the Spirit, but the one great constant has been the beautiful feelings that have accompanied the love and tears we've shared."

—Barry and Lucie Gibbons

$\mathcal{T}$AKE NOTE

"When I was young, I remember being surprised at how many friends at school wished me a happy birthday. I was amazed by how many people knew that it was my birthday, and wondered how they had found out. I didn't find out until third period, when I changed for gym class and noticed a note taped to my back, written in Mom's handwriting, that said, 'Today is my birthday. My mom wrote this note, so don't tell me it's here.' What a fun surprise! Every year, Mom always looked forward to sneaking a note onto our backs as we headed out the door for school."

—Jeffrey M. Loveridge

$\mathcal{H}$AVE IT YOUR WAY

"We have a birthday cake that is decorated the way the honored person wants it to be—sometimes the children even decorate the cakes themselves. Inside the birthday cake are several coins (wrapped in clean foil). It is fun to see who gets the money when the cake is cut."

—Janet Dunford

$\mathcal{M}$AGIC BIRTHDAY

"When someone in our family turns the same age as their date of their birthday, we call it a 'Magic Birthday.' This means that they will receive as many presents as the age they are turning. For example, if they turn nine on the ninth of the month, they will receive nine gifts."

—Randi Nuila

THE LION HOUSE

"I think we all can look back on a time, sometime in our youth, when Mom tried to surprise us with a party. I remember one day walking home from elementary school, and Mom stopping by to pick me up in her car. When I looked in the backseat, all my friends were there, and they all yelled 'surprise!' Mom then took us to the Lion House, where we had a wonderful birthday party, complete with pioneer stories, taffy pulling, and sugar-covered seagulls. I loved my birthdays growing up, but the surprises were always the best."

—Carrie N. Loveridge

BOMBS AWAY!

"After every present-opening ceremony in the family, we somehow have gotten in the habit of wadding up the wrapping paper and tossing it at one another. These 'wrapping paper fights' have become a fun way for the family to wind down after the party."

—Michael Dustin

BIRTHDAY REUNION

"Because many of our children and grandchildren live out of town, we have a big 'family reunion' type birthday party. The children enjoy going out together, and in the evening, the adults go out to dinner. After both occasions, we all come back to my house for birthday dessert."

—Beverly Glade

Put It in Writing

"I always write a special letter to the birthday person acknowledging his or her particular accomplishments during the past year."

—Pauline Whitehead

Reminder Binder

"I keep a binder to remind me of all the family's birthdays throughout the entire year. Inside, I keep a year's worth of cards so that I can just pull them out, sign them, and deliver them to all of my loved ones on their special days."

—Denise Wright

General Family Fun

The great thing about traditions is that you don't even need to have an occasion to warrant a fun activity. Our family loves to dive into different family activities—spontaneous or planned—without having a particular purpose for getting together. We have found that we don't need a specific holiday for creating memories as a family; we just need time together.

Book Trade/Exchange

For those who have favorite books, have a potluck dinner with extended family and instruct all who attend to bring some of their favorite books that they are willing to loan. After dinner, take turns giving a mini synopsis of books, and loan the books to those who want to read them over the next month or two. If you have books you're willing to part with permanently, place them in a pile for each family member to "shop" through. It is a great way to recycle the books and still keep them in the family.

Be a Reading Family

Keep a book in the glove compartment of your car, and every time you go someplace as a family, read to each other. You can also read books to each other in the evenings. Over the years, you will read many classics and have a wonderful time together sharing and discovering new horizons.

Secret Service

Once a month for family home evening, choose a widow or single person to receive your secret "surprise" service. Decide on the activity, such as raking leaves, washing windows, trimming shrubs, cutting the lawn, or weeding flower beds or gardens, or all of the above! When you show up with rakes, gloves, shovels, and hoes, you will delight the person you've chosen to receive your service.

Family Quilt

Have family members create individual quilting blocks to make quilts for newlyweds or new babies in the family. Precut the squares and allow enough time for the family members to make something nice. When the blocks have been sewn together, involve others in helping to sew the binding to add their share of the service.

A Celebration of Life

"My teenage daughter, Julie Ann, was killed in an automobile accident twenty-five years ago. Her father and I spent nearly one hundred hours sorting and scanning pictures and writing Julie's history to share with the rest of the family. I personally felt her spirit as I worked on her story. We presented each of our children with their own copy of 'The Celebration of Julie's Life.' We all felt a warm spirit as we viewed the books, and we reflected on the gospel truth that families are forever."

—Charlotte W. Zarkou

Family Song

Choose a familiar song that all members of the family know, and write new words to it about your family. Include different verses for every member of the family, making sure to name some of the unique characteristics of each. These songs will become cherished and will certainly fill the halls as the family members go about their business.

COMPLIMENTARY APPLIANCES

Place a bulletin board on the fridge with a section for every family member. Keep a pen handy. Throughout the week, encourage family members to notice something nice about other family members that they could write down and tack on the board. At the end of the week, sit together as a family and read aloud all the special things you have noticed about one another.

BOOKWORMS

Take your children to the library often. This alternative to television can instill a love of books and a lifetime habit of reading. It's the perfect activity when the children think there's nothing to do.

SATURDAY FAMILY ACTIVITY JAR

Have your children choose ideas for fun activities they want to do on the weekends and write them on pieces of paper. Then, each week, take turns pulling a slip out of the jar after the chores are finished. The whole family agrees to participate in the activity of the week.

HOMEMADE KITES

Plan to fly kites as a family. However, add a special touch by making the kites yourselves. Cut tissue paper and glue it onto a cross-shaped frame for a kite; then have the children draw their own designs. Go to the park on a windy day and fly your creations.

Backyard Golf

Build a homemade mini golf course in your backyard. Dig small divots out of the grass with a bulb planter, and put them back in after the game. Have a tournament with prizes for all who participate. Maybe nobody will get a hole in one, but this game is truly a winner.

"Drive-in" to the Garage

Take your television out to the garage to create a family "drive-in," complete with popcorn and drinks, where you can watch a favorite movie. Kids can make "cars" out of cardboard boxes with pillows to sit on while watching the movie.

And I Quote . . .

Have a special notebook in a handy place so that every time someone reads a particularly poignant, humorous, or interesting quote, they can write it down in the notebook. It's a great place to go for ideas when the time comes to give a talk or thought.

Our Motto

Choose a saying or motto for the family and display it during the week. Have family members recite it every day to ingrain the thought into their minds. One friend told her children that they were the "Happy Family," and they heard this often. One day, she overheard her child telling his friends that he belonged to the "Happy Family."

Bread Bar

Get together with your extended family, when possible, and have everyone bring a special loaf of bread. Bring jam, butter, and honey for all to enjoy the homemade treats.

Gimme Some Skin

Create a family handshake. Kids will love to help think up some "moves" for hand slapping and finger snapping that your family can do together. It will be fun, whenever family members accomplish something special, to give them the familiar family handshake.

Talent Sharing Night

Have a family talent show. Make it a special night, and have the children dress as they would for a professional concert. Allow each child to announce his or her own number and to enjoy an individual moment of glory in front of the whole family.

Service Scavenger Hunt

Make a list of simple tasks that can be done at neighbors' homes and send your family on a scavenger hunt, performing services for neighbors. Neighbors must sign when the job is completed, and can sign for only one job per home. Set a time limit and have prizes for the fastest workers.

Bean Jar

Challenge the family to do secret acts of service for one another. Whenever people complete a service, they tell Mom, who gives them a bean to put in the "service jar." When the beans reach certain levels, such as one-fourth or one-half full, take the whole family out for a reward. When the jar is full, have an extra special night out together.

Traveling Video

This is great for extended families who live far apart. Have one member start a videotape, taping family scenes for about fifteen minutes, and send it to the next person. They will then add their fifteen minutes and forward the tape. After the tape has been filled and everyone has been included, make copies for each individual family to have its own record of that time.

The Cookie Drawer

"The tradition of our cookie drawer began nearly forty years ago and continues today. We keep a drawer in the kitchen stocked with cookies, and the neighborhood children are free to come over and knock on the door anytime to be invited to the cookie drawer, where they get to pick 'one for each hand.' Even the teenagers have stopped by over the years, using the cookie drawer as an excuse to seek some counsel and encouragement."

—Ardeth Kapp

Welcome to Our Neighborhood

Whenever someone new moves into your neighborhood, teach your children the importance of fellowshipping. Have your family help prepare a treat to take to the new people; then have the children come with you to deliver the treats and introduce yourselves. It would also be helpful to include a list of other neighbors' names and phone numbers, schools, stores, trash pick-up information, and other useful hints about your area.

Music Appreciation

As a family, attend local musical and dramatic performances. These may be professional events or simply high school plays and concerts. Talk together about what you have seen and learned. If the performance involves music only, teach the children to make mental pictures as they listen and to try to feel the peace and beauty of instrumental music.

At Grandpa's House

"My grandparents had a tradition of having the grandchildren over for sleepovers from time to time. The night was filled with pizza, soda, and games. Because there are so many cousins, we usually had two groups for the sleepovers, one for the older kids and another for the younger children. Those sleepovers with the family provided some of my greatest memories."

—Nonie Marshall

Happy Birthday, Bach!

To gain a better appreciation of classical music and composers, celebrate the birthdays of the men and women who created beautiful music. Have an evening of listening to several pieces and reviewing the composer's life and accomplishments.

Cookie Bouquet

Have fun making different shapes of sugar cookies and decorating them to make a bouquet for someone in the family. For example, if a person is starting a new job, you might make cookies to look like dollar bills, dollar signs, or other things that pertain specifically to that job. You can do this for birthdays, starting school, or any other special occasion. Roll the cookie dough thick, and stick a small dowel or barbecue skewer in the bottom of each cookie for a "stem" as soon as the cookies come out of the oven.

Thankful For . . .

"Every night before family prayer, we went around the circle and had each person say one thing they were thankful for. This became a habit in our family when I was just a toddler. Because I got so used to this tradition, I insisted that we do it every night of my childhood. Occasionally, when we were a little rushed before family prayer and tried to skip it, I recall reminding the family, 'Wait, we have to do "thankful for."' And we always did."

—Amy L. Hendrickson

Savings Supper

"After we have accumulated a lot of fast food coupons and they are about to expire, we put the kids in the car and take along paper plates, cups, and napkins. Then we drive from one fast food place to another, ordering only what we can get with the coupons. We split the hamburgers and drinks. It is a blast and a great way to eat out without spending a lot of money."

—Kay Cannon

We Thank Thee, O God, for a Prophet

Take time to celebrate the birthdays of Church Presidents, past and present. Make a cake and sing "Happy Birthday" to them. Acknowledge the current prophet by sending birthday wishes on homemade cards. Include a special note of gratitude for his years of service and inspiration.

Baptisms for the Dead

"One of the most special times with our family was going to the temple to do baptisms together. We have come to the point in our own family's genealogical research where names are hard to find, so we got family names from a friend. It was great to be there for someone else's family, and to help them by this service, but it was also significant that we were there together as a family."

—Jennifer L. Dustin

I'M GOING THERE SOMEDAY

Take the family to the temple on a Saturday morning in the summer when there will most likely be newlywed couples outside having their pictures taken. Talk to the children about their goal to be sealed in the temple, making sure to point out the joy on the faces of the couples and their families.

KID'S DAY

"It always seemed a little unfair to the children in our family that there was a Mother's Day and a Father's Day but not a Kid's Day. So we decided that we would institute a Kid's Day to be celebrated on the first Saturday in June. On Kid's Day, the entire family does whatever the children decide, such as going to the zoo or to an amusement park."

—Christian Meyer

THE STORY THAT NEVER ENDS

"Reading to children brings a closeness that can extend beyond the early years. Throughout our childhood years, my mother read the newspaper to us as we ate breakfast. I always enjoyed the time of having someone else read to me, and I still love to have stories and articles read to me as well as reading myself."

—Robert E. Hales

Off with the Old, On with the Old . . .

Have a get-together with extended family members at which each person brings clothing that he or she has outgrown. Hold each item up or lay them all out on tables and have the family members choose the "new" clothes that they will take home to their own closets.

Family Game Night

"We get together every three months or so with the entire extended family and have a big game night. It is great to get together with everyone, to keep in touch, and to share some laughs as well."

—Julie Knapp Meyer

Here Comes the Sun

"Every summer we plan a sunrise celebration. We wake up while it's still dark and sit on the back lawn to wait quietly for the sun to rise. We talk about our blessings and then have a big breakfast in the early morning sunshine."

—Kay Cannon

Name Them One by One

In family prayer, take the time to mention individually each family member and something specific to his or her needs or talents. This will help everyone in the circle understand the important place each person fills in the family, and will increase their love for each other.

Rainy Day

"Every time it would storm in the summer, Mom would cut up a cantaloupe and sit with us on the front porch. We would wrap up in blankets and listen to the rain while eating our treat. Even though most of us are grown, whenever it rains, someone still suggests that we cut up a cantaloupe and go outside to sit."

—Tiffany L. Johnson

We Are the Kings

"At a family home evening, our family created a theme, which we recite often together. In it, we listed our goals and values and our conviction of who we are. As the children go out the door, I remind them who they are by asking them, 'What are Kings?' and they respond by repeating our family theme."

—Kevin and Amy King

Family Harmony and Getting Along

Like every family, ours definitely has its share of not-so-peaceful times. We have found that it takes a lot of effort on everyone's part to maintain a positive spirit in the home. We try many different methods of creating peace and harmony, and all of our family members enjoy the blessings of our extra efforts.

ARGUMENT ARIAS

"We had a rule in the home that if any of us had something to 'discuss' with another family member, we had to sing our argument. We are not all particularly musically talented, but somehow this always brought out the opera singer in us. It also scared away any contention that might have otherwise accompanied the confrontation."

—Carrie N. Loveridge

A SOFT TOUCH TURNETH AWAY WRATH

When there is a sensitive subject to be discussed between family members, have them hold hands as they work things out. The gentle touch of a hand will certainly help the discussion go more smoothly and more sweetly.

THERE'S NO PLACE LIKE HOME

If there seems to be a lack of harmony in the home, make sure that the children are not allowed to leave or go to a friend's home. They will learn that they must get along with family members and work out their problems instead of running away from them.

SING A HYMN

It is amazing how an outside observer can help change the mood in a tense situation by simply singing the first phrase to "Love at Home."

Xoxoxo

After every family prayer, have each family member hug, kiss, and say "I love you" to every other member of the family. Even when there are disagreements, that simple gesture at the start and finish of every day will keep the spirit of love and harmony close by.

Never a Negative

Whenever the tone in the home changes and someone starts to say something negative, teach the entire family to clap twice at hearing something that isn't conducive to the Spirit. It can be a bit of a game, but more importantly, it will stop negativism in its tracks.

Let the Punishment Fit the Crime

There is nothing like a little bit of service to soften the heart. Whenever there is a disagreement or argument in the family, have the offending person perform a significant act of service for the person he or she has offended. They will soon learn the value of getting along!

To Quarrel Is to Clean

If you find your children in an argument, simply hand them a broom. It will not take long for them to realize the value of discussing things in a gentle and calm manner and of working things out for themselves without involving the parents.

Eleven Commandments

"Mom created 'the eleven commandments of the house' that hung on our wall in the kitchen. They were simple instructions that all of us were to obey regarding dispositions, chores, and other items. I particularly liked the first one, which she copied from a friend: 'Thou shalt be cheerful. Be witty if you can, be pretty if you are, but be cheerful if it kills you.'"

—Jennifer L. Dustin

Screech to a Halt

It seems like parents all too often ask, "Do I have to turn this car around?" when their children are fighting in the car. Once in a while, it wouldn't hurt to actually do it. When children realize that their vacation or outing hangs by one behavioral thread, they will certainly be more compliant to Mom and Dad's wishes to get along in the car.

The Happy Place

"Whenever my children forget themselves and are particularly whiny and sulky, I have them sit on the 'happy blanket' until they can find their cheerful dispositions again. This works wonderfully well and reminds the children that our home is a place of happiness."

—Tiffany L. Johnson

Television and Computer

As a family, we have found that our relationships are neglected when the television and computer take up most of our time. When we limit our time in front of the screen, we increase the time available for us to do things together.

Television Fast

Get rid of the television completely for a month. Children will soon have to find other means of entertainment, and family members will have more meaningful interactions with one another. Best of all, you will all realize what a waste of time television can be and will become more sensitive to the declining moral values portrayed on today's shows.

Grounded from TV

It's amazing how dependent children become on their favorite television programs. It seems that the television could become a negotiation ground for parents who want more out of their children. When children quarrel or fail to complete their homework, for instance, you could "ground" them from watching television for a certain period of time.

Reruns

In a society of declining television morals, it is often hard to know what programs portray the same values that your family treasures. You might want to take time to prerecord some old shows that you feel comfortable having every member of the family watch. *The Andy Griffith Show, Leave It to Beaver, Father Knows Best,* and *The Dick Van Dyke Show* are all favorites.

Pay-Per-View

If the television seems to be turning into the central focus of all entertainment in the home, institute a system of payment whereby the family must "buy" time to watch. This might be through actual monetary means, or may be by trade through chores, homework, or cheerful dispositions.

A Time for Everything

Limit the amount of time that children spend on the computer and in front of the television. It weakens interactions when children bond with a screen instead of with the family. Decide as a family how much is enough, and then monitor closely to make sure that nobody in the family exceeds his or her quota. Daily passwords for the computer work well to help control computer use.

An Eye for an Eye

Have a deal with the family members in which each hour of work gets them one hour of television. Or, for a variation, have each homework assignment allow them one television program. You might also try trading one "educational" program for each "cartoon."

Bedtime

We have found that bedtime is a terrific time to build closer relationships with our children. Some of our best conversations with family members happen at bedtime. As the very last event of the day, our bedtime rituals serve as a calming, peaceful, and even spiritual experience just before we fall asleep.

ℋ Tape to Sleep With

"Bedtime is a special time of day for our children. My husband and I have made our own tapes with each of us telling stories, singing songs, and doing other activities like counting or reciting rhymes. When it's time for our children to go to bed, we sit with them for a while, and then they listen to our voices on the tapes until they fall asleep."

—Jan Marshall

ℙillowcase Prayers

You can purchase "glow-in-the-dark" paint that will not wash out in the laundry. Give the children fresh, new pillowcases and have them use this kind of paint to write down something on the cases that will remind them to have their personal prayers. At night, when they turn out the lights, the reminder will "glow" and they will remember their prayers.

ℬedtime Express

At bedtime, after family prayer, make a "family train." Line up, and have each member of the family hold onto the waist of the person in front of them. Make "choo-choo" sounds as you trek through the house to each child's bedroom. At each room, have the family hug that person good night, and then trek off to the next child's room. This family farewell is certain to bring sweet dreams.

A Rocky Reminder

Take the family outside and let each member select a good-sized rock. Wash the rocks and paint them in bright colors. Have the children place their rocks on their pillows, so that when they go to lie down at night, they will see the rocks and remember to say their prayers.

Pajama Jam

Each night at bedtime, play a familiar tune for all the family to hear that signals time to get their pajamas on. They have only until the end of the song to change into their pajamas and be in the family room for prayer.

Lullaby and Good Night

In the half hour or so before bedtime, play lullaby music throughout the home to let the children know that it is now quiet time, a prelude to bedtime. This creates a calm mood that will help the children wind down from their day.

Prayer Rugs

"I bought some small carpet squares and painted a stencil of a child praying in the corner. I gave one to each of my grandchildren to put by their bedsides to remind them to say their personal prayers. My children have told me that their children are certain at prayer time to run and sit on their prayer rugs."

—Diane Bytheway

CLOSING TIME

"In our home, the whole house shuts down at the same time. For the younger children, it means bedtime, but for the older children, it means that they must now retire to their own bedrooms for some quiet time. The central parts of the home are 'closed.' This makes for a relaxing night for the parents because we now know that all the children are in their rooms."

—John Bytheway

LEARNING THE HYMNS

"At bedtime, each child gets a back scratch and a song. Because I sing hymns to them each night, they learn them easily, and whenever they hear a hymn I have taught them, they have fond memories."

—Sharlene Hawkes

A PERSONALIZED SONG

"At bedtime, my mother would sing 'Dearest Children, God Is Near You' (*Hymns,* no. 96). She would insert the name of whomever she was singing to in place of the word *children.* She would stroke our hair as she sang to us. No matter what else was going on, I felt all was right with the world when my mom sang to me."

—Amy King

A Nontraditional Afterthought

As if we haven't already shared enough, we just wanted to express one more point. Traditions are wonderful, and they will truly serve to bring your family closer together and to strengthen relationships. However, the activities and events that we call our traditions are only the means of travel, not the destination. You don't get together for gingerbread-house decorating so that you can all have a delicious treat to enjoy (although that is one of the sweeter side benefits). The real purpose is the interaction and strengthening of relationships.

Before you know it, your family will be grown. Your children will be getting married and joining with their new spouse's family as well, who will most likely have their own set of family traditions. Your married children may not always be able to come to every Easter egg hunt.

They might be able to join you only every other year on Christmas. That's all right. They are teaching their own children new traditions and sharing in the traditions of *both* sides of their family.

It's important when possible to maintain those family traditions that have become such an important part of your lives, but it shouldn't become so important that those traditions strain the very relationships that they have served to strengthen. Sometimes traditions need amending according to differing family needs. Traditions should grow and change, just as the family grows and changes.

Finally, enjoy! There is much love, joy, and laughter to be found in the time you spend together with your family as you create and carry out your own wonderful traditions.